DANGEROUS GROUND

THE WORLD OF HAZARDOUS WASTE CRIME

DONALD J. REBOVICH

WITH A NEW INTRODUCTION AND EPILOGUE BY THE AUTHOR

Transaction Publishers

New Brunswick (U.S.A.) and London (U.K.)

New material this edition copyright © 2015 by Transaction Publishers, New Brunswick, New Jersey.

Copyright © 1992 by Transaction Publishers, New Brunswick, New Jersey.

This book is printed on acid-free paper that meets the American National Standard for Permanence of Paper for Printed Library Materials.

Library of Congress Catalog Number: 91-18199
ISBN: 978-1-56000-014-3 (cloth); 978-1-4128-5601-0 (paper)
Printed in the United States of America

Library of Congress Cataloging-in-Publication Data

Rebovich, Donald.
    Dangerous ground : the world of hazardous waste crime / Donald J. Rebovich. p. cm. Includes bibliographical references and index.
ISBN 1-56000-014-7
    1. Offenses against the environment—United States. 2. Hazardous waste disposal industry—United States—Corrupt practices. 3. Hazardous wastes—Law and legislation—United States—Criminal provisions. I. Title.
HV6403.R43 1991
364.1'42—dc20   91-18199
                                                                      CIP

DANGEROUS GROUND

In Memory of Mary Isabelle Mullin

Contents

Preface

It wasn't too long ago that most of us considered *waste* to be a common term describing all types of "garbage," making no distinction between fairly innocuous and dangerous wastes. Conventional wisdom held that the ultimate destination of all waste was the local landfill. Not many gave a second thought to the chemical properties of industrial wastes mixed with household wastes dumped at the landfills. If business firms were caught dumping their wastes, it was treated as more of a nuisance rather than as a criminal act. Simply put, the common images of the criminal and the dumper were worlds apart.

We have come a long way since that time; both in terms of public awareness of the dangers of hazardous waste exposure and our willingness to accept the notion of the criminality of improper disposal. A series of ecological disasters caused by the irresponsible storage and dumping of hazardous waste has compelled us to reevaluate our thoughts on the criminality of environmental violations and has prompted our legislators to enact tough new criminal laws intended to curb these unscrupulous acts. It has now become the job of federal, state, and local law enforcement officials to see that these laws are uniformly enforced—no small task considering we know very little about who the polluters are and how they commit their crimes.

A primary objective of this book is to provide empirical information on characteristics of hazardous waste crime and the criminals themselves. Regrettably, the research community, much like the community at large of the past, has paid very little attention to hazardous waste criminality. States wishing to mobilize rigorous criminal enforcement programs have been unable to turn to research studies that could provide them with a foundation for proactive, investigative operations. In this book, I provide a historical analysis of hazardous waste crime enforcement up to the present, an assessment of hazardous waste crime and enforcement data from a number of states, projections of future patterns of hazardous waste crime, as well as some thoughts on what we can do to limit the peril posed by unchecked criminal dumping. This information will, I hope, prove to be useful in helping to target offenders and to make it less difficult to bring them to justice.

As a society, we have learned that our most damaging crime problems, such as drug abuse, cannot be ameliorated through law enforcement efforts alone. We now recognize that such problems are most effectively dealt with by focusing our attention on causation issues as we seek to establish meaningful methods of deterrence. Such is the case with hazardous waste crime. Unless we are willing to seriously explore and adopt alternatives for waste source reduction, waste recycling, and the realistic availability of legitimate waste disposal outlets, we will reduce hazardous waste crime enforcement to an exercise in futility. With this thought in mind, I caution that the information supplied in this book will be most valuable only if what we have learned is coupled with openness to new ideas on the legitimate reduction/disposal of hazardous wastes.

I am indebted to a number of colleagues who supported me through the completion of this work: David Twain, James Finckenauer, Todd Clear, John J. Gibbs, Michael Greenberg, and Freda Adler. I am particularly thankful for the guidance given to me by the late Richard Sparks. He was the source of direction for subject conceptualization and for the selection of research methods.

It is with great pleasure that I also acknowledge the considerable support I received from the New Jersey Division of Criminal Justice and the Northeast Hazardous Waste Project. Special thanks go to Robert Robillard, Linda Tartaglia, Wayne Fisher, Thomas O'Reilly, John Holl, Steve Madonna, James Lyko, Keith Wellks, and Philip Ahrens. The environmental law expertise of Peter Crane Anderson proved invaluable in the description of the legal structure of the states studied.

The two individuals who provided me with the most gratifying personal support were my wife, Mary Mullin, and my son, Nikolas. I thank my wife for urging me on to complete the product you now have in your hands and for overlooking my changes in temperament as I struggled to be creative. She always had great patience with me, constantly encouraging me with the words, "Don, you can do it."

Introduction to the Paperback Edition

This book is about hazardous waste. More specifically, the book is about what hazardous waste is, how it is generated, how it is legitimately treated, and, especially, how and why it is so often illegally disposed. The book answers questions such as: Who are the offenders? What drives them to commit these offenses? What are the most common methods used for committing the offenses? How do these offenders attempt to avoid criminal enforcement detection? How successful are these individuals in getting away with these crimes? The book also shines a spotlight on the efforts used to control and deter environmental crimes involving hazardous waste. It addresses the questions here regarding: What are the government agencies responsible for controlling illegal hazardous waste dumping? Who are the people within these agencies who are entrusted with carrying out these responsibilities? What factors influence effective crime control methods? How can we enhance our abilities, as a society, to reduce hazardous waste crime commission in the future?

This book was first published at a time in which environmental crimes were making national headlines throughout the country, particularly in the northeastern United States. Groundwater was being contaminated by the wanton dumping of hazardous wastes in secluded areas. Hypodermic needles and other medical wastes were washing up along the Atlantic Coast shoreline. Spectacular fires and explosions were taking place at industrial sites where hazardous wastes were being illegally stored and disposed. One of the burning questions that was being posed at the time by the media was, Who "masterminds" these types of offenses? Some concluded that the strings were being pulled by members of syndicate crime organizations. However, little empirical research had been conducted to objectively examine characteristics of environmental crimes and criminals. This new edition of *Dangerous*

Ground recounts the lessons learned from the original research and places that knowledge in the context of national and international developments in the present-day world of environmental crime.

This book is a chronicle that supplies answers to the questions posed above. It is, in effect, an account of the first empirical study of environmental crime cases over an eight-year time span. The study focused on disposed environmental crime cases from the state attorney general offices of four states that had been seriously victimized by environmental crimes; Maine, Maryland, New Jersey, and Pennsylvania. At the time, typical wastes being illegally disposed of in these states were petrochemical wastes, electroplating/metal treatment wastes, and galvanizing wastes. In New Jersey, some of the most serious offenders were found to be treatment, storage, and disposal facilities, (TSDs) designed to provide the means for the legitimate treatment and disposal of hazardous wastes. While at present, some new waste sources have gained prominence in recent hazardous waste crimes (e.g., "fracking" wastes, wastes entailed in the illegal disposal of electronic devices, coal mining wastes), the methods used to commit these offenses and attempt to avoid detection, have largely remained the same.

The book starts with a chapter that addresses the definitional basics of the hazardous waste term and a discussion of the elements that make up "hazardous waste." It goes on to describe national efforts to confront the growing problem of ground and water contamination resulting from the unscrupulous actions of handlers of hazardous waste material. This leads to a discussion of the Resource Conservation and Recovery Act and the transition of environmental civil offenses into the criminal justice arena. This introduction sets the stage for explaining how hazardous wastes can be legitimately treated before disposal; the processes that criminal dumpers typically avoid.

From this starting point, the book's narrative then takes the reader into an explanation of the primary objectives of the study the book is based on and the mechanics on how the study was actually implemented. From there, the book highlights the main findings of the study regarding key characteristics of hazardous waste crimes and those who commit them. Some of the most prominent results include how the study found the average offender to be a variation of an ordinary, profit-motivated businessperson who becomes a "criminal opportunist." These individuals become criminals because they recognize and capitalize on criminal opportunities presented by lax enforcement and ample seclusion areas often provided by features of the natural environments of the four states studied. Offender types are depicted as covering a wide range from line level truck drivers who actually dump the wastes up to executives who have a major part in the approval of illegitimate methods of disposal.

The study results explain how some of the keys to success for the skillful environmental offender include a sense of "knowledge." This knowledge may be the understanding of how natural environments might present challenges to environmental enforcers in discovering the offenses and tracking them to the offenders. In addition, the findings uncovered explain the formal and informal relationships between regulators and those who are regulated, and how the offenders are able to expertly evaluate the vulnerabilities of regulation systems and regulators themselves, aggressively attacking the weak points that are exposed. This can include honing skills in "detection avoidance" by simply visualizing a "picture" that no one else seems to see (e.g., a blighted landscape, pockmarked with boreholes descending to abandoned coal mines). Such a landscape can look very different to an enterprising environmental offender. To this person, the desolate landscape represents a potential criminal "bonanza."

The findings go on to explore the dynamics within the environmental criminal groups that describe apprenticeship systems of criminal conversion including the structure of covert reward systems. The results presented enlighten the reader on how offenders understand that the methods of illegal disposal should become "moving targets" that can position them one step ahead of those responsible for enforcing the law. Inventive methods employed by offenders demonstrate how environmental offenders can be considered criminally astute "innovators." Special attention is paid to how hazardous waste crimes can occur within small, informal networks of waste generators, waste transporters, and employees of treatment/storage/disposal (TSD) facilities. As depicted by enforcement experts interviewed, results help explain how efforts by criminal syndicates to infiltrate this arena have failed largely due to features of criminal commission methods and to the fragmentation of hauling and TSD firm interests. In addition, the book reveals how TSD facility offenses were often committed under approval of executive officers of the facilities who turned to illegal disposal as a response to their inability to manage proper waste treatment economically.

Besides providing a critical analysis of environmental crime characteristics and environmental offender characteristics, a chief objective of this study is to assess the types of investigations that occur and how the investigations can overcome obstacles that may stand in the way of effective investigation and prosecution. Attention is paid to the means of discovery of environmental crimes, important sources of information that lead to detection, as well as prominent surveillance methods used. The results describe some of the public and corporate pressures that can be put on environmental prosecutors associated with cases involving the illegal disposal of hazardous wastes.

Dangerous Ground concludes with a discussion of a follow-up survey of hazardous waste enforcement representatives from the four study states, as well as ten other eastern states, with regard to changes in trends for characteristics of hazardous waste crime. Recommendations are offered on the redesign of enforcement to make it more proactive, the enhancement of inter-governmental cooperation to improve enforcement effectiveness, regional approaches to hazardous waste crime enforcement and new paths for sanctioning strategies. For the private sector, suggestions are offered on the importance of the facilitation of imaginative waste reduction/treatment methods for the future. In addition, the author offers insights into how environmental crime has changed in the twenty-first century and how control efforts should adjust to these changes.

The study on which the present work is based was able to peel back some layers of uncertainty associated with hazardous waste crime and supply a more holistic portrait of the offense and the offender that, up until the first publication of *Dangerous Ground*, had been unavailable to the public. Illegal activities involving the handling and disposal of hazardous wastes persist today across the U.S. In light of often dwindling resources dedicated to environmental law enforcement, investigators continue to struggle to gain the competitive "edge" over those who would engage in illegal disposal activities that poison our ground and waterways. The hope is that this edition of *Dangerous Ground* will help open doors for future research of hazardous waste crime, will serve to reinforce the significance of this menace to our nation's health, and help promote endeavors to explore fresh approaches to containing this threat.

1

Beginnings of the Problem

For a thorough knowledge of the state of hazardous waste crime in the U.S., it is essential to determine what circumstances have led to our present catastrophic environmental conditions. Hazardous wastes have been produced as manufacturing by-products for many years. But the improper dumping of these materials has only recently been interpreted as so grave a threat as to warrant criminal investigation and prosecution on a wide scale.

Hazardous Waste: What Is It?

The term *hazardous waste* has been defined in a variety of ways since the public has become familiar with the term. In the Resource Conservation and Recovery Act (1976), Congress supplied a legal definition that classifies hazardous waste as any refuse that

> because of its quantity, concentration or physical, chemical or infectious characteristics may—(a) cause, or significantly contribute to an increase in mortality or an increase in serious irreversible, or incapacitating reversible illness; or (b) pose a substantial present or potential hazard to human health or the environment when improperly treated, stored, transported, or disposed of, or otherwise managed. (42, U.S.C., 6901–6987, 1976 & Supp. IV, 1980)

The Resource Conservation and Recovery Act (RCRA) also specifies eight variations of toxicity that can exist and, under most state law frameworks, must be proven in criminal prosecutions of hazardous waste offenses. The targeted wastes will cause the most harm to the environment and to human health through (a) surface water contamination, (b) ground water contamination via seepage, or (c) air pollution.

There is a wide range of sources that comprise hazardous waste generators in the United States. These are not only represented by the major petrochemical industries but also include the end-user, private homeowners who improperly dispose of household chemical cleaners and disinfectants every day. As we are reminded by those who have researched the effects of improper disposal, hazardous wastes can be categorized as a subset of by-products emanating from "manufacturing processes, scientific and medical research, discarded consumer products, diverse processes used in the delivery of services and a variety of other activities in the public and private sectors" (Greenberg and Anderson 1984, 1).

From the beginnings of the Industrial Revolution, technological innovations have given rise to special types of hazardous wastes as by-products. But it wasn't until petroleum was used as a primary ingredient for the manufacture of synthetic organic chemicals that the world completely recognized the significance of the resulting waste disposal issue.

Organic chemicals are those containing carbon, an element that links with itself to form chains of organic chemical compounds. In the post–World War II era, science was able to imitate the diverse characteristics of organic chemicals, forming the basis for products like plastics, electronic components, and construction materials, to mention a few. Since World War II, the nation's production of organic chemicals has rocketed from less than 20 billion to over 220 billion pounds a year. More than 380 billion pounds of solid hazardous wastes and 412 pounds of aqueous hazardous wastes are generated annually by this industry, making it the largest single producer of hazardous wastes (Sarokin, et al. 1985).

Options for the Disposal of Hazardous Waste

Corporate efforts to expand production and to explore new markets have complicated the problem of the growth in volume of these wastes since the 1940s. The economies of scale are enormous, especially for the petroleum industry, which uses expensive equipment. The pressure to cultivate new markets has led to the generation of new waste materials and the unfortunate compromising of ethics in the disposal of the wastes. The chemical industry has, consequently, been accused of shirking the responsibility for the proper disposal of wastes by claiming that, because society is the beneficiary of chemical products, it should therefore bear the brunt of the responsibility (Brownstein 1981).

We know that now, more than ever, major industries face increasing competition and the prospect of shrinking profits. But those generating the largest volumes of hazardous wastes are particularly financially vulnerable, as are small businesses pressed to set aside large percentages of assets to meet disposal regulation standards. The truth is that the cost of legitimate hazardous waste disposal has risen steadily since the

1940s and has been seen as a deciding factor for corporations choosing to dispose illegally.

Hazardous waste generators have a number of legitimate disposal methods open to them. Treatment methods like incineration, biological treatment, or chemical decomposition destroy much of the hazardous materials present in wastes. Hazardous materials treated with these methods are converted into innocuous substances like carbon dioxide or water. Recycling, reuse, and recovery practices are methods used by some generators. Although the legitimate landfilling of hazardous wastes has been minimized through Environmental Protection Agency (EPA) directives, the discharge of hazardous wastes is still permitted in certain forms. One of the more controversial forms of discharge is deep-well injection, in which toxic liquids are disposed a mile or more below ground (Westat Inc. 1984; Sarokin et al. 1985).

Unfortunately for waste-generating businesses, the costs for many disposal methods can be staggering. The cost of legal treatment of hazardous wastes can range from $15 to $550 per 55-gallon drum, depending on the chemical. Pharmaceutical companies average $125 per drum for proper disposal. Given these rates, it is not hard to imagine how dramatically profit margins can be increased by unscrupulous generators who, through illegal arrangements, dispose at a small fraction of the legitimate treatment cost (Krajick 1981).

The cheapest form of illegal disposal is a practice known as "midnight dumping"—a term as accurate as it is colorful—in which all that is required is "a truck and a lack of regard for public safety" (Wolf 1933, 441). Wastes are often disposed of in the nearest isolated area. Agents of generating companies can directly commit these offenses or criminally conspire with waste transporters or treaters who, for a percentage of the legitimate treatment cost, will illegally dump the wastes. In some instances hazardous waste generators become victims of fraud committed by midnight dumpers. In these cases, payment is rendered by the generator to the treater for services that are never performed (Krajick 1981). Other dumping patterns involve open storage in deteriorating dumps, disposal in insufficiently lined landfills, and burning in defective incinerators (Wolf 1983).

Early Government Response to Improper Disposal

Until the 1970s, government response to the growing menace of hazardous waste crime was perfunctory at best. The general public had not yet become collectively outraged enough to pressure the government to

3

act—that is, until one tragic event placed the hazardous waste problem at the center of media attention. Carson's fabled "city of silence" had suddenly become reality in the form of Love Canal.

In 1978 the entire nation learned of the Love Canal disaster, in which 263 New York State families were forced to abandon their homes because of conditions created by hazardous waste pollution. The dumping of the chemicals was conducted by the Hooker Chemical and Plastic Corporation and had actually begun decades before. Compounding the pressure on the government to respond was sharp congressional criticism of the EPA's ineffectiveness in limiting damage associated with the improper disposal of hazardous waste.

The response to the public clamor was Congress's passing of the Resource Conservation and Recovery Act. RCRA instructed the EPA to come up with a national manifest system for tracking hazardous wastes "from cradle to grave" and to structure violation penalties. In effect, the act was a regulatory overhaul of the hazardous waste management industry. The road to the Act's implementation was long and rugged because of administrative delays and technical problems. It wasn't until 1980 that the EPA was compelled to issue many of the RCRA regulations.

On the heels of the creation of the new RCRA regulations, Congress established a program to expedite the cleaning of most of the known hazardous waste dumping sites. The Comprehensive Environmental Response Compensation and Liability Act (CERCLA), established in 1980, came to be commonly known as "Superfund." It became apparent rather quickly that a superhuman effort was required to make the program succeed. Early noble intentions were rudely rebuffed by the hard realities of implementing such a monumental task. Five years into the program, less than 10 percent of the EPA's 850 priority sites had received any remedial attention. Part of the reason for the delay was that the program required substantial cleanup cost contributions by the states—50 percent for public property sites and 10 percent for private property sites—that could not be provided (Magnuson, 14 October 1985).

Both RCRA and CERCLA were early, conceptually sound strategies to bring the management and cleanup of hazardous wastes in line with the demands of an increasingly impatient public. Improper hazardous waste disposal was on the upswing in the America of the 1970s; it was clear that a strong government agency was needed to guarantee that the new laws were vigorously enforced. Sadly, the EPA would not meet this challenge, throwing the federal enforcement of RCRA and CERCLA, and the EPA itself, into a state of disarray that would last for years.

The EPA Enforcement Disaster

From the late 1970s to the early 1980s, the EPA was to be the target of much public criticism for the lagging progress of RCRA and CERCLA. Compounding the obstacles inherent in enforcing such sweeping acts, the EPA under the Reagan administration was accused of being overly cautious in dealing with violators. But the most serious damage to the EPA's approach to the hazardous waste crisis was yet to come. The damage was rooted in President Reagan's ill-fated selection of top officials to be entrusted with carrying out the agency's environmental mandates.

The EPA's enforcement and administrative credibility began to crumble shortly after a second Love Canal–type incident had seeped into the country's consciousness. In February of 1983 EPA administrator Anne Burford announced the $36.7 million federal buy-out of an entire town, Times Beach, Missouri, which had been contaminated by a waste hauler contracted to spray oil on streets to eliminate dust. The town's 2,500 residents were relocated and most of its businesses and homes sold to the federal government. It was in the wake of this second major hazardous waste calamity that the EPA began to feel the barbs of government accusations against its top officials (Schmidt, 25 February 1983).

By the end of February 1983, New Jersey Representative James Florio had accused the EPA of sanctioning the awarding of a $7.7 million cleanup contract to a company charged by EPA a month earlier for covering up pollution violations. Chemical Waste Management Inc. was found to have been represented by a lawyer, James W. Sanderson, who was a former consultant to then EPA administrator Anne Burford (AP, 23 February 1983).

Chemical Waste Management Inc. of Oak Brook, Illinois, had earlier profited from an EPA decision to dismiss a Federal ban on landfilling hazardous wastes. The disposal company was able to bury 1,500 barrels of hazardous waste before public outcry forced a resumption of the ban several weeks later (AP, 23 February 1983).

Sanderson was one of a group of conservative Republicans from Colorado who filled a number of important federal government positions on the environment in the early 1980s. The key appointments went to Coloradans like Anne Burford, her husband, Robert, head of the Bureau of Land Management, and then Interior Secretary James Watt (Schmidt, 25 February 1983).

5

During February 1983, the EPA scandal had resulted in the firings of several top officials, including the head of the EPA's hazardous waste cleanup program, Rita M. Lavelle. The EPA situation became even stickier when Lavelle asserted before a House Public Works subcommittee that the EPA was in chaos because of internal rivalries and had no formal structure of organizational command (Weisman, 21 March 1983).

Oral allegations by the EPA's top administrators of subordinate mismanagement were countered by subordinate retorts of upper management malfeasance. At the time, the head of several congressional investigations into the agency, Representative James Scheuer (D–New York), characterized the EPA as "a frightened administration, unable to stop the hemorrhaging . . . now attempting to limit the bad news by killing off its messengers" (AP, 24 February 1983).

Under investigation by a half-dozen congressional committees as well as by the Justice Department, Anne Burford resigned her position in March 1983. As the congressional committee's work went on, further damaging information about the management of the EPA surfaced. The head of the agency's Midwest regional office admitted to doctoring an EPA report that had blamed Dow Chemical's Midland, Michigan, plant for dioxin contamination (Shabecoff, 16 March 1983).

Burford and her top EPA officials were spared from criminal indictment. Rita Lavelle wasn't as lucky. In August 1983 she was indicted on five felony counts, including perjury before congressional subcommittees. Four of the counts resulted from her testimony to three subcommittees concerning her obstruction of an EPA investigation involving her former employer, Aerojet General Corporation (Weisman, 21 March 1983).

The House Energy and Commerce Committee's Oversight and Investigations Subcommittee concluded its report on the management of EPA under Burford in August 1984. The report charged that high level officials of the EPA had violated their public trust by (1) manipulating the Superfund cleanup program for political purposes, (2) engaging in unethical conduct, and (3) generally disregarding the country's public health and environment. Specially, the report asserted that Burford and Lavelle had purposely limited expenditures to clean up abandoned waste sites to dissuade congressional extension of the cleanup program (AP, 30 August 1984).

Efforts to Quell the Storm

President Reagan eventually turned to his first administrator to try to restore order and integrity within the EPA. The selection of William

D. Ruckelshaus momentarily took some of the political sting out of the preceding scandalous events at the EPA. Ruckelshaus was praised by environmentalist and business groups alike as an intelligent choice. His efforts to restore order and public confidence in the troubled environmental agency drew praise from some congressmen. But others were less satisfied (Weisman, 21 March 1983).

Some public officials and environmental activists lamented that Ruckelshaus had been unsuccessful in persuading the Reagan administration to improve its record on policies relating to groundwater safety and pesticide pollution, among other issues. While Ruckelshaus did demonstrate greater tenacity in attempting to solve the country's hazardous waste problems, his performance fell short of early optimistic hopes (Weisman, 21 March 1983).

Under EPA administrator Lee Thomas, the agency made some strides toward improving its image. But worries still persisted about the EPA's ability, or willingness, to protect the nation's health against the consequences of improper hazardous waste disposal. If one is to judge by a 1989 report by an EPA inspector, there remained reason to doubt that the agency had come close to its full potential of effectiveness. In February 1989 an EPA inspector general reported that the EPA had rewarded a Superfund cleanup site-inspection contractor for work not up to par and kept some northeastern region inspection experts confined to office work for nearly a year. The inspector general's report went on to explain that employees held back from making site inspections, and had resorted to conducting mock exercises to preserve their skills in sampling hazardous wastes. In place of traditional site visits, inspectors were advised to rely on state agency files or data from consultants contracted with companies potentially responsible for improper disposal (AP, 23 February 1989).

The Shifting of Enforcement Responsibility

Ann Burford's administration during the early 1980s remains a dark chapter in the history of the EPA. For those of us seeking to learn more about industrial hazardous waste crime characteristics, however, it is important not to understate the impact this period had on shaping those characteristics. The EPA during the early 1980 set the stage for a brand of enforcement of hazardous waste dumping that in many cases actually provided rich opportunities for the commission of these violations.

EPA enforcement activities were cut back significantly during the early 1980s. Between 1980 and 1981 the EPA's Office of Enforcement experienced a 69 percent decline in cases referred to the Justice Department and an 82 percent decline in RCRA and Superfund cases. Because EPA enforcement, in many ways, serves as a model for state environmental protection agencies, the EPA's lack of enforcement aggressiveness during the Burford years had a trickle-down effect on many of these agencies, allowing offenders to operate unencumbered by fear of detection. Lack of resources and adequate training, combined with mission ambiguity, further diluted the effectiveness of regulatory enforcement at federal and state levels (Metz 1985).

Matters have improved since the days of the Burford scandal. But there still exists a dichotomy of compliance monitoring and criminal enforcement that underlies many state hazardous waste enforcement programs. One of the cornerstones of the EPA's enforcement policy since 1983 has been to delegate operation of environmental enforcement to the states. A chief goal of a large number of these programs is to initiate regulation compliance by hazardous waste generators/handlers through manifest self-monitoring or through government inspections (Metz 1985).

The states that have taken a step in the war against hazardous waste crime are those that have formed task-force partnerships between state environmental protection agencies and state attorney generals' offices. These states have proven that the task-force approach can be successful even though philosophical differences may arise between inspectors advocating monitoring compliance and criminal enforcers promoting harsher forms of deterrence.

Subsequent chapters will explain how several northeastern states plagued with hazardous waste crime mobilized regulatory and criminal enforcement resources to reverse past enforcement failures. These states developed some of the first hazardous waste crime task forces in the United States and, like the EPA, encountered problems posed by lack of resources. The story of their enforcement experience is central to the first empirical search into the world of the hazardous waste offender.

2

The Search for the Hazardous Waste Offender: Past Works

Since the post–World War II era, we have seen the sweeping growth of the major hazardous waste producing industries, the marked rise in waste management costs, and the sometimes callous disposal of these materials in unorthodox fashions. We have also witnessed the damage such dumping has had upon the environment and human health, and the official recognition of this problem as being of such gravity as to warrant federal and state legislation and specialized criminal investigations and prosecutions. Sadly, little effort has been expended on researching and identifying characteristics of the hazardous waste offender in hopes of learning more of his operative style and criminal associations to facilitate proactive enforcement aims and to enhance criminological knowledge of this phenomenon.

Most of the early published material on hazardous waste crime dealt with Superfund legislation and waste-generator liability (Brenner 1981; McPheeters 1980). Pecar (1981) has berated the field of criminology for virtually ignoring the subject of ecological offenses even though the consequences of such crimes in many ways cause more harm than other forms of deviant behavior. Still, attempts have been made to define some dimensions of the hazardous waste offender.

Reports by Mustokoff (1981), Krajick (1981), and Epstein et al. (1982) have contended that hazardous waste crime often yields "perks" to part-time transporters who may or may not conspire with generators or waste treaters. Intimations have also been made (Blumenthal, 5 June 1983; Epstein et al. 1982) that hazardous waste offenders actively solicit the aid of both legitimate and illegitimate "outsiders" who are, seemingly, indispensable for the successful commission of offenses. Some authors have reported that a major portion of hazardous waste crime involves the criminal behavior of the waste generators themselves, usually agents of corporate enterprises (Blumenthal 1983; Mustokoff

1983). Some allege a combination of corporate naiveté regarding environmental damage, corruption, and regulatory inefficiencies as the chief causal factors (Epstein et al. 1982). Others are less charitable to the generating companies. Wolf (1983) asserts that industry often attempts to exonerate itself by rationalizing that, in the past, generators were ignorant of the possible damage caused by their disposal methods and did not expect contracted disposal firms to dump improperly. Wolf questions these explanations and implies that industry has consciously disregarded potential harmful consequences in their quest of reduced disposal costs. Probably one of the most ambitious works attempting to define the hazardous waste criminal was a 1986 study by Szacz. In it, the author gives his interpretation of the interplay between hazardous waste generators and treatment/storage/disposal (TSD) facilities offering criminal services and explains how regulatory structures permitted these relationships to exist.

Szacz parallels TSD industry of the northeastern United States with that region's solid waste disposal industry; he presumes that hazardous waste treatment, storage, and disposal is, like the solid waste industry, dominated by syndicate crime interests and is run through a "property rights" system of cartel manipulation. In Szacz's scenario, the hazardous waste TSD industry is organized such that both competition within the industry and the contractual choices of hazardous waste generators are severely restricted. Further, Szacz concludes that hazardous waste generators participate in what he calls an "externalizing criminogenesis" whereby "actors from a totally different world, the underworld," accept responsibility for illegal disposal activities that would normally be assumed by the generators. It is this purported connection between syndicate crime and hazardous waste crime that forms the basis of what has proven to be the most controversial by far of all writings on the hazardous waste criminal.

The "Poisoning for Profit" Controversy

In 1984, William Morrow and Company published *Poisoning for Profit: The Mafia and Toxic Waste in America,* a book that was to be a tinder-box in the hazardous waste/syndicate crime connection arena.

Co-author Alan Block was then an associate professor of criminal justice at the University of Delaware and had produced a number of scholarly works on organized crime. His associate, Frank Scarpitti, was at the time of the book's publication a professor of sociology at the University of Delaware. The author of many books on a variety of criminological subjects, Scarpitti had once served as the president of the American Society of Criminology. Their book follows the evolution of the hazardous waste glut as a social problem on a national scale, from the implementation of RCRA to flaws in manifest tracking systems to the entrance of the hazardous waste hauler.

The heart of the book, and the focus of much controversy, was the authors' claim that illegal hazardous waste disposal was operated and controlled by the mob. Primarily addressing hazardous waste crime in New York and New Jersey during the late 1970s, the authors describe a process of syndicate exportation from the states' solid waste industries to their hazardous waste industries. According to the authors' findings, syndicate operatives, leading lucrative lives of crime in the solid waste industry, expanded their criminal interests by infiltrating the hazardous waste treatment industry. The bottom line, as put by Block and Scarpitti, is that syndicate crime holds the country's future hostage by controlling hazardous waste trade associations as well as those responsible for enforcing environmental laws. Law enforcers are taken to task for what is seen as their failure in this area. The authors insinuate that hazardous waste criminals would not be as successful as they have been without overt collusion by politicians and law enforcement officials.

The publication of the book set off a chain of events that neither the authors nor the publishers expected. A series of lawsuits were brought against the publisher by individuals and organizations cited in the book. One such suit was filed by Waste Management, Inc., for allegations connecting the organization with syndicate crime. Another lawsuit was lodged against Block and Scarpitti by the former director of New Jersey's Division of Criminal Justice, Edwin Stier.

Stier contended that Block and Scarpitti had unfairly characterized him as corrupt and his organization as having protected hazardous waste criminals. In a settlement reached between Morrow and Stier in February 1986, the publishing company agreed to recall all copies of the book and promised not to reissue it without advance inspection by Stier. The settlement with Waste Management, Inc., was in a sense more damaging to the book: the authors issued an apology and an admission that their sources of information had provided them with erroneous information. Subsequently, Morrow destroyed the entire inventory of *Poisoning for Profit*.

The controversy surrounding *Poisoning for Profit* was not confined to the two lawsuits. The Academy of Criminal Justice Sciences had showcased the authors and their research at the Academy's 1984 annual conference. The research was lambasted by an academy member, Frederick Martens, in the academy's September 1985 newsletter, which precipitated an exchange of accusatory letters between the authors' and Martens' follow-up newsletters. The spillover of the controversy into the academic community drew additional attention to this initial description of the world of hazardous waste crime, and to the methods of data collection (Martens, September 1985).

Block and Scarpitti's analysis was conducted at a point early in the evolution of hazardous waste crime investigation, when duplication of enforcement operations, by fragmented enforcement agencies, was commonplace, as were interagency disputes over the suitability of those methods. Unfortunately for Block and Scarpitti, they selected investigative sources who were later found to have personal motives for accusing government officials of malfeasance. Corruption charges made by these sources during House subcommittee hearings were ultimately refuted or satisfactorily explained.

Despite the surrounding controversy, the authors' important questions remained viable, and unanswered: How much hazardous waste crime is syndicate crime? Why did hazardous waste crime become so prevalent during the 1970s and 1980s? What roles did government officials play in these crimes? After the debacle of the only major work on hazardous waste crime, those searching for answers to these questions were back to square one.

3

An Empirical Approach to Hazardous Waste Crime Research

Despite the increased scholarly interest in hazardous waste crime, there have been few works specifically focused on the environment of the offender himself. Our knowledge of the hazardous waste offender's world thus remains limited.

Companies that generate hazardous wastes naturally have a relationship with those responsible for its treatment, storage, and disposal. A more intricate set of relationships—as this study will show—exists among members of the workplace up and down the hierarchy. The allure of the hazardous waste crime workplace for incoming personnel, especially lower-level employees will eventually place some of these workers among the population of hazardous waste offenders. The stronger the allure, the greater the organization's ability to sustain its systematized criminality over time.

To arrive at an understanding of the activities, events, and associations characteristic of hazardous waste crime and criminals, this study undertook a contextual analysis of the criminal offenses, including methods of commission, skills required for commission, degree of offender participation in other crimes, use of legitimate and illegitimate outsiders, links to syndicate crime, and the corporate levels of waste-generating offenders. Also examined were investigative and prosecutorial styles, and the way in which both the formal and informal patterns of social control help to mold official offense and offender characteristics.

The following topics and research questions provided the framework for the study:

- Occupational Characteristics
  — What types of firms are most commonly charged in cases of hazardous waste crime?

13

- — What are the most common professions of individual offenders charged with hazardous waste crime?
- — At what hierarchical level do individual offenders operate within the firm?
- — Do individual offenders commit offenses for personal gain or do they represent the interests of the firms?
- Methods of Commission
  - — What are the most common methods of commission of illegal disposal of hazardous wastes followed by criminally charged offenders?
  - — Have these methods demonstrated modification over time?
- Levels of Professional Crime
  - — What is the extent of criminal backgrounds of criminally charged offenders?
  - — To what degree do charged offenders participate in hazardous waste crime as part of a criminal "career"?
  - — Do hazardous waste offenders enter into the treatment/disposal industry with the *intention* of disposing illegally and/or defrauding generators?
  - — In what ways are criminal careers in the hazardous waste treatment/disposal industry developed?
  - — What technological skills of hazardous waste treatment/disposal do criminally charged offenders possess?
- Levels of Organized Crime
  - — To what degree are criminally charged offenders recognized as members of highly organized syndicate crime?
  - — How prevalent are criminal conspiracies (group crime) in the commission of hazardous waste offenses?
  - — How prevalent are intrastate and interstate criminal networks?
- Crime Control Response
  - — What are the investigative/prosecutorial techniques most commonly used in the attempted control of hazardous waste crime?
  - — What are the most serious obstacles to the effective investigation and prosecution of hazardous waste offenses?

Organized Crime: A Continuum Approach

There has been much discord in the criminology field as to the most credible conceptual definition of organized crime. Probably the most generic definition is offered by the 1976 National Advisory Commission on Standards and Goals. The commission describes organized crime as being represented by

> any group of individuals whose primary activity involves violating criminal laws to seek illegal profits and power by engaging in racketeering activities and, when appropriate, engaging in intricate financial manipulations ... the perpetrators of organized crime may

include corrupt business executives, members of the profession, public officials, or members of any occupational group, in addition to the conventional racketeering element. (213).

The National Advisory Commission's definition is commonly accepted as a definition of *group crime*, that is, crime committed by two or more people. Hagan's content analysis of selected criminologists' definitions of organized crime, published in 1983, reveals a more narrowly defined and realistic conception of organized crime. Hagan found that most of the selected criminologists were in agreement with Albini's (1971) core definition of *syndicate crime*, in which the organization uses or threatens force, supplies profitable illegal services that are in high public demand, and assures immunity of operation through corruption. Hagan's refined definition of syndicate crime is the more commonly accepted definition of organized crime; it excludes many examples that the group crime definition includes: "For example, corporate criminals while involved in some 'illegal enterprises' are predominantly involved in legitimate operations and are generally less likely to resort to violence on as systematic a basis as syndicate criminals" (53).

The drawback common to both definitions, as pointed out by Hagan is that they are limited to identification only: is it organized crime or isn't it? A more fruitful approach, as Smith suggests (1980), would be to judge *to what degree* something is organized crime. Smith recommends a continuum model that would measure the degree to which an organization can be considered an illegal enterprise. Such a continuum, created by Hagan (1983), cites the "costa nostra," "mafia," or "Italian-American syndicate" as a prototype that would represent the highest degree of organized crime. Those groups falling below this prototype on the continuum would be defined as "semi-organized" or "loosely organized" crime not possessing all the features of organizational "hierarchy"—restricted membership, secrecy, violence or threats of violence, provision of illicit goods and/or services, and immunity through corruption.

By applying this continuum approach, one can judge in which areas a given group is strong or weak, hence discerning to what degree it can be considered organized crime in the purest sense.

This study follows Hagan's lead and strives to determine the degree of organized crime along a continuum. In past discussions of the subject, the discriminating quality of analysis thus afforded has been absent. (See Appendix A for discussion of past related works).

Hazardous Waste Crime as Professional Crime

An additional study aim was to ascertain the extent to which hazardous waste offenders conform to the commonly held definition of *professional crime*. Are the offenders inclined to perform their illegal activities as part of full-time "careers," or to indulge in merely ancillary rewards of otherwise legitimate businesses. An associated question is, To what extent do offenders require skills fundamental to the commission of the offenses and that could only be acquired by industry functionaries? Interview data gathered by Epstein, et al. (1982) suggest that a great deal of illegal hazardous waste dumping is likely to be conducted by a small number of people who are technologically adept in disposal methods and who are skilled in developing businesses that satisfy licensing standards. Also, according to their interview results, the companies with seemingly honorable reputations are often discovered to be the most unscrupulous offenders.

Is the hazardous waste professional offender part of a totally criminal subculture where occupational conventionality would be considered a deviation and lead to peer ostracism? Is he a conventional businessman whose criminality is an outgrowth of occupational concerns and objectives, and who views highly visible associations with known criminals as undesirable?

A key aim, then, of the present study was to ascertain to what measure hazardous waste offenders conform to the commonly held definition of "professional crime." In effect, this raises the question of whether the offenders are inclined to perform their illegal activities as a full-time "career" or if they indulge as merely an ancillary reward of an otherwise legitimate business. An associated issue here is to what extent offenders require knowledge of skills fundamental to the commission of the offenses that could only be acquired by industry functionaries. Interview data gathered by Epstein et al. (1982) suggest that much illegal hazardous waste dumping is likely to be conducted by a small number of people who are technologically learned in disposal methods and who are skilled in developing businesses that satisfy licensing standards. Also, according to their interview results, the companies with seemingly honorable reputations are often discovered to be the most unscrupulous offenders.

Sutherland inaugurated the term "professional crime" in the path finding book, *The Professional Thief* (1937). The work is an analysis of the criminal careers of thieves based on commentaries of thieves and descriptions of their activities. Sutherland contrasted their field to professions in the conventional business world and typified their professionalism as encouraging (a) technical skills, (b) a sense of status, (c) a sense of organization, (d) a sharing of a common code of ethics and language, (e) a systematic use of connections to deal with emergencies, and (f) differential association. Of critical significance here is that Sutherland portrayed the professional thief as necessarily being trained by other professional thieves. Since Sutherland's study, scholars have developed variations on the original operational definition of the professional criminal. Inciardi's (1975) definition dictates that one can become a professional criminal only if one has been inducted into the world of crime before entering any conventional occupation. Inciardi further imparts that "his" professional criminal does not pursue a legal course of occupation at any time for this would jeopardize his criminal status within his professional crime subculture. Gould, Bittner, Messinger, Powledge, and Chaneles (1966) totally abandon the concept of skill in their operational definition of professional crime. They loosely interpret professional crime as not demanding a specialization of skills and pictured them as generalists who may conceivably associate with other like offenders but are devoid of any professional devotion or allegiance to them or to any ethical code.

Letkernann (1973) adopted a more middle-ground stance with his interpretation by stressing levels of professionalism based on rankings of acquired skills. He also suggests the offenders are not philosophically constrained, as Inciardi would have us believe, but will actively seek out conventional approval beyond what can be bestowed by other professional criminals. The breakthrough "Study of the Causes of Crime for Gain" (Sparks, Greer, & Hanning, (1982) unearthed valuable information in its delineation of the significance of both learned skills and group support. The authors explained how skills are involved in most crimes for economic gain, the meaningfulness of technological constraints in determining forms of criminal organization, and the genesis of group support in the commission of these offenses. Aside from perceptual skills employed in "casing," the writers' findings support the views articulated by Klockars (1974) and Levi (1981) that submit that skills required for the acquisition of property in crime for gain are skills that can be learned legitimately and, indeed, often are. This conclusion is significant for it opposes the postulate projected by authors like Inciardi (1975) who insist that such skills are learned as part of a criminal milieu that engulfs the actor's actions.

The present study adopted a position on an operative "professional crime" definition that addressed the issue from a continuum perspective similar to Hagan's organized crime definition. That is, instead of encumbering the study's decision-making mechanisms, and consequently forwarding a myopic version of professional crime, the present study closely allied with Letkemann's tack and concentrated on determining to what degree hazardous waste offenders can be viewed as "professional."

Hazardous Waste Crime as Work Place Crime

Reports by Mustokoff (1981) and Krajick (1981), and Epstein et al. (1982) have revealed that much hazardous waste crime may take the form of part-time "perks" of transporters who may or may not conspire with generators or waste treaters. Examinations of similar types of "part-time" occupational crime have found that they can be highly organized or can be individualistic and are characteristic of a wide array of occupations (Ditton, 1977; Henry, 1978; Mars, 1982). A recognition of these authors' findings provides a helpful guide toward a thorough analysis of part-time crime and the social arrangements that offenders promote to commit the unlawful acts. Mars (1982) professes that these 11 part-time" criminals, or "fiddlers," hatch ways to bend the rules so that they might cultivate "covert reward systems" for themselves as a riposte to insufficient salaries and/or as a retaliation to the perceived inequitable systems imposed by employers and/or regulators. Mars deduces that "total reward systems" for such "fiddlers" are the coalescence of formal legal rewards (wages, salaries, commissions): informal legal rewards (perks, tips, extra work); and illegal rewards (overloading, pilfering, returns from professional crime) He also sees the attainment of a desirable "total reward system" often requiring covert arrangements with other workers or outsiders. It is the regular presence of total reward systems and the networks of work-based social relationships through which total rewards are differentially allocated to individuals by what is termed individual contracts that are the "covert institutions" of occupational life.

Classification of "fiddlers" and their characteristics is produced by Mars' study and divulges that "fiddlers" do not simply abscond with what materials are available in an undesigned mode but recognize certain rules of commission. These rules dictate the identity of those who are eligible for "fiddling," those who could be incorporated in a "fiddle," and limitations on amounts of gains. The "fiddlers'" occupations are classified by "grid" and by "group" dimensions. Those jobs that restrict worker autonomy through inflexible regulations and task expectations are considered "strong-grid" jobs while an absence of viable constraints typifies "weak-grid" jobs. "Strong group" occupations demonstrate high collectiveness and subordination of the individual worker to the work group and reciprocal actions, and responsibilities between the community at large and the individual worker. "Strong group" occupations are linked to frequent contacts between co-workers that transpire in a mutually interconnecting network and often expand beyond the workday environment.

Conditions that favor the permanence of "fiddles" and allow them to flourish are recounted by both Ditton (1977) and Mars (1982). They introduce examples of occupations where fiddles are positively reinforced by co-workers and, in some cases, where workers are actually coerced into participation. Some "fiddlers" exploit their supposed professional "expertise" by duping unwary customers into paying for a service not rendered. In "triadic" fiddles, a customer and an employee may ally against the employer, or the employer and the employee may collude to deceive the customer (Mars, 1982). Ditton (1977) exemplifies this latter situation in his unfolding of how baker's deliverymen are trained by management to compensate for unavoidable shortages on delivery rounds by swindling customers. This is viewed as an acceptable practice by deliverymen since the accounting system is such that shortages become inevitable.

Trust relations are frequently forged in the social milieu of "fiddling," trust relations that complement the more formal transactions indigenous to the profession. These relations are dubbed the "amateur trade" of "fiddling" by Henry (1978) and usually take the form of worker A directing an "extra something" to worker B who is then expected to reciprocate when an opportunity is presented and with whatever arises. This social arrangement is further bonded for worker B will now anticipate, at some future point, that worker A will offer an ill-gotten gain to worker B as a cyclical continuation of the "amateur trade" (Henry, 1978).

The works of Henry(1978), Ditton (1977), and Mars (1982) are valuable to the present study for their discoveries help shape research questions on the characteristics of work-place crime. Surface parallels exist between Ditton's and Mars' depictions of triadic offenses and known hazardous waste criminal events (Krajick, 1981; Mustokoff,1981). The utility of the authors' findings assists the present study's design in assessing how similar hazardous waste crime is to other forms of work-place crime. In short, the study explores how conditional hazardous waste crime is on management and work group control, the worker's perception of occupational rewards, pressures to participate in "fiddling," the strengths of "amateur trade" networks, and opportunities for fiddling. A value of this study is that it concomitantly illuminates the nature of "fiddle proneness" of the hazardous waste disposal industry.

Hazardous Waste Crime and Fraud

Based upon disclosures by Krajick (1981), Mustokoff (1981), and Epstein et al. (1982), a share of hazardous waste offenses involves some systematic defrauding of waste generators. In these cases, transporters and/or treaters of hazardous wastes accept payment for services that are never legitimately performed. Treatment agencies have been known to stockpile drums of waste and abandon the operations after going "bankrupt"(Krajick, 1981; Wolf, 1983). A case study approach to elucidating this specialized style of fraud, in an area apart from hazardous waste crime, was done by Defranco in Anatomy of a scam—A Case Study of a Planned Bankruptcy by Organized Crime (1973). Records of court testimonies were studied to help highlight organized crime's actions of gaining control of a legitimate business and driving it to bankruptcy. Profits are reaped by initially purchasing merchandise on credit, transforming the merchandise into cash, and milking the cash from the business after which the company is "forced" into involuntary bankruptcy by its creditors.

A more wide-reaching study of those businessmen who defraud their suppliers is furnished by Michael Levi in The Phantom Capitalists (1981). In the report Levi painstakingly describes the social and organizational characteristics of "long-term fraud." Through the analysis of data collected from interviews with a number of convicted fraudsters, some unconvicted ones, businessmen, and law enforcement personnel, Levi was able to present a thorough review of fraud in which a business orders large quantities of goods on credit at a time when the owners of the business either intend not to pay for them or suspect that they may not be able to pay for them.

Levi was able to present a thorough review of the fraudster's world. He compiles an exact account of the social, moral, and technical organization of long-term fraud and a portrait of social reaction toward this crime. Levi contends that his findings are of significant criminological import for the following reason: "the people who commit it possess far more heterogeneous backgrounds than do most convicted adult property criminals. This offers us an unusually wide range of motivations for and organizational techniques of crime." (p. 3), In his book, Levi manages to categorize three principal types of long-term fraud. They are:

1) pre planned frauds which are businesses set up with the intention from the very beginning of defrauding suppliers;
2) intermediate frauds which occur when people decide to turn a formerly legitimate business into one which defrauds its suppliers;
3) slippery-slope frauds which occur when businessmen continue to trade and obtain goods on credit although there is a high risk that unless their business situation improves greatly, they will be unable to pay for the goods.

Levi (1981) was able to frame the structure of pre- planned long-term frauds by constructing organizational typologies and describing their operations through their interrelationships and through relationships with law enforcement personnel. Levi found that a particular type of pre-planned long-term fraud known as "villain fraud" enjoys a high degree of organizational differentiation, largely to reduce the risks of identification and conviction for the principal organizers. Levi found that "villain fraudsters" follow functionally distinct roles even though the same individual may fill a number of them. Levi's interview data also permitted him to piece together four principal modus operandi of pre-planned fraud.

In his concluding summary of the social and criminal organization of long-term fraud, Levi argues against Sutherland's (1937) discussion of the professional criminal in which Sutherland contends that one cannot become a "professional thief" without receiving one's education through association with other thieves (pp. 197–198). Levi argues that such "differential association" is unnecessary for the crafty businessman and actually may be a hindrance. Except for previously laid-out references to the current state of knowledge on the defrauding of hazardous waste generators, little indisputable data have been uncovered about the underlying properties of this phenomenon. It is especially speculative as to whether such fraudsters are otherwise legitimate waste treaters who intermittently engage in fraudulent enterprises or whether their criminality is embodied within preconceived schemes that constitute the solitary purpose of their agency's creation. Levi's study (1981) demonstrates a firm grasp on the translation of evidence of the defrauding of suppliers into functional classifications that should augment the current study's exploration into: (a) types of hazardous

21

waste fraud, (b) types of roles played by hazardous waste fraudsters, and (c) levels of associations with other known criminals.

"Outsider" Networks

Intimations have been made (Blumenthal, 1983; Epstein et al., 1982) that hazardous waste offenders actively solicit the aid of both legitimate and illegitimate "out siders" who are, seemingly, indispensable for the successful commission of offenses. The present study's investigation into this inference requires a thorough examination of the organizational environment that could help identify environmental forces that have the power to set limits to and expand criminal activity discretion. This demands a description of methods in which waste generating corporations, waste haulers, and waste treaters may recruit "significant outsiders" in the "task environment." Of interest here is the way in which toxic waste offenders form coalitions with local politicians, regulatory agencies, and other "outsiders" to effectively complete offenses.

The present study measures how closely findings align with Levi's (1981) analysis of the villain fraudsters' environment where functionally distinct roles are assumed by such "outsiders" and the same individual may fill more than one role. Sparks et al. 's work (198 underscored the importance of ancillary tasks and those who afford them. The Sparks et al. (1983) study accentuates the importance of not only the criminal "project" task itself, but also the pivotal nature of the many ancillary tasks that, without their presence, would jeopardize the triumphant completion of the chief criminal action. These ancillary tasks are identified as including, most notably, the furnishing of alibis by others, critical materials, and the disposition of stolen property. Their work goes on to note the primacy of the interrelationships of those comprising small, but critically utilitarian, networks to ensure criminal activity fruition. The authors are careful to state that they believe that as commercial and industrial processes evolve, so will evolve the skills needed to carry out the crimes and so will evolve the interrelationships of the criminal actors.

"Shaping" the Legal Environment

The "outsiders" who play a meaningful role in hazardous waste crime commission have sometimes found to be regulation officials themselves. While the public-at-large may conclude that regulatory agencies operate without the consent of the agencies they regulate, there is much historical evidence to refute this belief (Hopkins, 1979; Kolka, 1963).

The creation of the EPA has been seen as a response to environmentalist and consumer persuasion but corporation evoked pressures have still surfaced as a potentially viable force of environment "shaping." Clinard and Yeager aptly note that the issuing and enforcing of regulations, in contrast to the common legal system of the separate enactment of laws by legislatures and the application by courts, are both responsibilities of regulatory agencies. This leaves the regulatory agencies vulnerable to corporation pressures regarding both legislative and enforcement functions. "When such influence is disproportionately strong, as compared with that of other constituencies, the agency's regulatory mission may be sacrificed in favor of corporate interests" (p. 106).

Clinard and Yeager explain that many regulatory agencies demonstrate some evidence of succumbing to corporate influence peddling and consequently, at times, enter into the business of protecting rather than regulating corporate actions. The corporate success of this influence is not necessarily attained through "arm twisting" but through much subtler means. Regulatory exposure to seminars, dinners, and junkets is a common method of "conditioning" regulators to the economic characteristics of the corporation and also their needs and problems. Often, in time, original legislative, executive, and popular support of the regulatory agency's efforts diminish when attention has shifted to more urgent issues of the day. (Clinard & Yeager, 1980).

The most overt of the subtler methods of influence involves the tempting of regulatory officials with promises of generous corporate positions upon reassignment from their regulatory positions. Such promises can be quite successful in diluting regulatory actions against them by keeping regulators mindful of how zealous enforcement can negatively affect future career prospects (Clinard & Yeager, 1980) Besides the tempting of regulators to compromise their positions, the assumption of corporate positions by former regulators holds a side benefit for corporations. Such individuals are often valuable to the agency due to the expertise they have accumulated in the particular industry and its bureaucracy (Vaughan, 1983).

The political arena has certainly displayed no immunity to the seductive advances of corporations. Promised corporate employment after government service is here, too, a temptation offered to politicians in exchange for actions decisions favorable to the industry. More direct forms of influence peddling have traditionally taken the forms of illegal contributions and legal but unethical contributions to politicos. Clinard and Yeager (1980) note that the Watergate investigations unveiled the extensiveness and form of illegal corporate contributions at the Presidential level.

In total, illegal contributions to the 1972 Nixon campaign entailed more than 300 major corporations (Clinard & Yeager, 1980). Although Clinard and Yeager express that the enforcement and regulatory agencies, developed in answer to environmental concerns, would seem to exhibit less evidence of succumbing to illegal and/or unethical corporate temptations, the topic remains a virtually untread field in hazardous waste generation research. Based upon the findings of past explorations of corporate influencing prac tices, a picture of the world of hazardous waste crime commission would be incomplete without a consideration of such corporate efforts to "shape" the surrounding legal environment.

Levels of Corporate Liability

A distinct genre of hazardous waste crime compromises the criminal behavior of the waste generators themselves, usually agents of corporate enterprises. Their wrongdoings can include the direct disposal of hazardous waste or the conspirings with transporters and/or treaters to dispose illegally(Blumenthal,1983; Mustokoff, 1983). It is debatable, however, how prevalent corporate criminality is within hazardous waste crime or at what corporate level it is most rampant. An awareness of corporate level responsibility is pragmatic for prosecutorial charging interests and also for forwarding corporate crime study. The present study therefore embraces this as an additional research issue.

Uppermost among the most important studies of corporate criminal responsibility is Clinard's interviews with 64 retired Fortune 500 middle management executives. Corporate Ethics and Crime (1983) centered on: (a) reasons some corporations are more ethical than others, (b) the influence that top management policies have on corporate ethics, (c) the impact of corporate pressures on illegal or unethical behavior, (d) ethical traditions of specific cor porations, (e) the tendency for middle managers to report corporate violations to the government,(f) the impact of competitive practices on violations, and (g) perceptions of government regulation and self-regulation. Clinard selected middle managers as his subjects due to the assertion that it is they who are ultimately responsible for carrying out top management directives.

The interviewed executives gave generally favorable ratings to ethical standards of their industries but in answer to more specific questions regarding ethics they presented evidence somewhat to the contrary. Fifty-three percent believed top management was the primary explanation for corporate violations through personal greed or through unethical behavior serving as a model. Ninety-two percent felt the top management set the ethical tone for the whole corporation. The same percentage felt top corporate executives should speak out publicly against illegal and unethical corporate behavior. However, 77% believed such officials should not speak out against a specifically named corporation. Within these 77%, some felt that this should not be done because it would be breaking some "unwritten rules" of the corporate game. In regard to pressures on middle managers, 78% of the respondents believed that work pressures led to the commission of illegal acts by middle managers. Respondents overwhelmingly reported that they would not report corporate incidents of price fixing, illegal rebates, and kickbacks or illegal payments to foreign officials mainly because such practices are customary in the corporate world. Of special interest is that nearly three-quarters of the respondents believed top management knew about corporate violations either before or after they occurred due to open lines of communication.

However, Stone (1975) points out that top management often purposefully engages in a self-imposed isolation from knowledge of misdeeds through their formation of reporting arrangements with subordinates. Carrol (1975) suggests that top management is frequently honestly unaware of middle management's unethical and illegal practices that are committed for the "good" of corporate objectives. In any case, the level at which true responsibility for corporate offenses is borne is still open to question. Clinard (1983) expresses that it is not always a simple job to discern where this responsibility lies: "When offenses are committed in a corporate context, individual executive responsibility is hard to assign. It is not an easy task for enforcement staff to deter where the responsibility and the authority to insure compliance with a specific law or regulation lie, so great is the diversification and so complicated the power structure of any large corporation. Often, top executives argue, they cannot be held responsible for acts they did not authorize and about which they have no specific knowledge. Such a defense is fostered in the corporate environment in the sense that middle management might often know what top management wants without their having to ask." (p. 157)

Patterns of Social Control

It would be short-sighted to conclude that the characteristic composition of officially known hazardous waste offenders is in no way a by-product of the nature of formal social control dominating the environment. The present study would, therefore, be negligent if it presumed a true contextual analysis of hazardous waste offenses excluding the patterns of investigation, arrest, and prosecution engendered within each sample region. Probably the most enlightening aspect of Levi's study is his empirical application to the study of substantial property crime of the ideas advocated by Cohen (1977) and Mcintosh (1975, 1976).

They maintain that criminologists have generally neglected the investigation of how "crime" is shaped by features of social organization and the system of policing. It is obvious that a primary goal of Levi (1981) was to: emphasize throughout the interaction between the practical organization of the underworld, the commercial world and criminal justice agencies, in a way that is absent from the few existing British studies of major property crime. The present study follows the path set forth by Levi and, thus, presents an exhaustive picture of not only offense/offender characteristics but also the official control mechanisms in place that can color its interpretation.

Mustokoff (1981) reaffirms that the industrial environment of corporate crime lends confusion to the issue of at what management level there is criminal liability and the question of whether it is most appropriate to prosecute the corporation or individuals employed by the corporation. Up until the landmark case of New York and Hudson River Railroad v. U.S., 292 U.S. 481 (1909), the prevailing concept was that corporations could not assume criminal responsibility. In the 1909 Supreme Court decision this concept was reversed. As Mustokoff explains, a corporation is most appropriately prosecuted as the defendant when the law violated specifies "absolute" or "strict liability." In such cases there is no need for the prosecution to prove motive, intent, or knowledge. However, many criminal cases are prosecuted against corporations for specific intent crimes committed by employees. The corporation can be held liable for criminal actions committed by upper level managers who have acted on behalf of the corporation but are generally not held liable for similar acts committed by mid-level employees. Here, the prosecution must show that the corpo-rate agent was acting within the scope of his authority and his action was not intended to benefit him but to benefit the interests of the corporation (Miller, 1980; Mustokoff, 1981).

Mustokoff (1981) believes that the most effective prosecution of corporate cases involving hazardous waste offense should also include the prosecution of individual corporate agents. The U.S. v. Park, 421 U. S. 658 (1975) Supreme Court decision developed the concept of the responsible corporate officer in which the President of Acme Markets was held responsible for violations of the Food and Drug Act. Responsibility was attributed to the corporate agent because it was decided that it was his responsibility to prevent the violations from occurring. Thus it is clear that individuals are responsible and accountable for any act done in the name of the corporation as well as the performance of any corporate - duty imposed by law. As in the Park case, it is not necessary for the individual charged to have participated in the crime, or even to have consciously done wrong. (Mustokoff, 1981, p. 57) The question of the appropriateness in the prosecution of corporations/corporate agents is not an easily decipherable one.

The current study *empirically* distinguished the distribution of prosecutorial choice, throughout the hazardous waste offense sample in the charging of: (a) the corporation, (b) the individual worker within the corporation, or (c) both corporation and agent together. These data expose the most common level of corporate responsibility in this crime area, the most popular prosecutorial strategies used, as well as the degree of success of these strategies.

Technological Competitiveness with Offenders

In adopting Sutherland and Cressey's (1970) perspective of "processes" in criminal behavior, there are some grounds to believe that enforcement lags behind waste offenders in the competitive development of technology. Preliminary investigative accounts have surfaced some initial evidence that presents methods of illegal disposal which have become more imaginative than in the past. Mcintosh (1975) has postulated that an organization's "criminal technology" is dependent on given opportunities for crime and given techniques for crime prevention. The current study shows that small groups have formed to ply their criminal trade in networks and the communications within these networks have developed to a degree that strive to lessen the odds of effective enforcement discovery. The usefulness of this knowledge would be aimed at those states that are not as up-to-date as other states in their efforts to constrict the "enforcement gap" through improved technology.

An exposure to the more intricate criminal methods could have a significant preparatory value to these states. In addition, such data would add greater texture to any attempt to identify important characteristics of the waste offender's environment.

Sources of Data

The present analysis of the hazardous waste offense/offender follows a research design that combines content analysis of case documents with interview surveys. The content analysis was conducted on 71 case files of disposed hazardous waste offense, interview information was obtained from 21 state law enforcement personnel who specialize in hazardous waste enforcement.

The study sample was drawn for all hazardous waste criminal offense cases[1] completed between January 1, 1977, and January 1, 1985, from the attorney general offices of Maine, Maryland, New Jersey, and Pennsylvania. A follow-up study was completed through the Northeast Hazardous Waste Project. To update study data from 1985 to the present, the follow-up study surveyed enforcement personnel from the original four sample states plus personnel from the Northeast Project's other nine member states.

The original three Mid-Atlantic states and one New England state were chosen from among 13 member states of the Northeast Hazardous Waste Project for three main reasons. First, three of the states (Maryland, New Jersey, and Pennsylvania) have exhibited a high concentration of known hazardous waste criminal offenses (i.e., offenses reported or detected) and, second, all of the sample states have displayed some of the most earnest systematic efforts in the United States to control these criminal offenses via state-level enforcement agencies. They therefore represent some of the best available material on hazardous waste criminal offenses within the context of a salient struggle to stem them. Thirdly, the three contiguous states were thought to be able to furnish data on any hazardous waste criminal networks that appear to operate beyond state borders. Maine was selected as a representative of a less industrialized state, and for its reputation for effective environmental enforcement.

As with most studies of criminal behavior, the degree to which unconditional, universal statements can be made about characteristics of offenders and offenses is inherently restricted by the practice of sampling. Sample cases are confined to those where criminal charges were lodged and where the resultant cases have reached disposition. The case documentation does not account for committed offenses unknown to authorities and that did not lead to criminal charges or for cases that have not yet been disposed. Therefore, the study's case file results cannot support indiscriminate generalizations about offenses/cases in these categories. Nevertheless, interview commentary does extend to all criminal investigations as well as to pending cases; thus its scope is somewhat wider than that of case file material.

Data Collection Strategies

The study's targets of analysis are hazardous waste incidents subject to formal criminal prosecution in the four indicated states. Within case files, all documentations of case processing (indictments, plea agreements); offense events (types of commission); offender communications (investigative interviews); and enforcement efforts (investigations) were examined. The study treats criminal cases as historical records in that it investigates the past social interactions among various types of hazardous waste offenders, and also the interactions among those offenders and the law enforcement community.

The interview questionnaires combined open- and closed-ended questions with emphasis on the former, given the exploratory nature of the study. In general, interview questions were guided by previously articulated hazardous waste crime issues reported by other authors (Blumenthal, 5 June 1983; Epstein, et al. 1982; Krajick 1981; Wolf 1983); by the unique objectives of this study; and by previously analyzed files. The open-ended construction of many of the interview questions allowed for the recognition of pertinent subjects unanticipated by the research plan as well as the effective analysis of common themes within responses.

The preliminary examination of case files served to refine, into general categories, information derived from investigative and prosecutorial memoranda, witness statements, pre-sentence reports, as well as other file materials. Close attention was paid to the relative frequency of documented presence or absence of organized crime contacts. Although this method of content analysis has been underused in white-collar crime studies, because of the lack of access to criminal case file data it lends itself well to the present problem.

Content analysis is primarily a coding operation whereby data is classified following some conceptual structure. Objectively identifiable phenomena, such as the number of regulatory violations and the number of bribes/attempted bribes per case, have been noted in the review process. The analysis of latent content (judgmental interpretation of data) is much more subjective because judgments are determined and coded rather than representing frequency of distinct activities and dispositions being objectively tabulated. Areas such as "types of service roles" and "types of services" were studied through a latent-content analysis. (See Appendix B for a more detailed discussion of research methods.)

Note

1.   This entails all nonpending cases in which individuals or corporations were charged with the illegal disposing of hazardous wastes, conspiracy to illegally dispose of hazardous wastes, or fraudulent schemes connected with the disposal of hazardous wastes.

4

Law Enforcement Structures of the Sample States

In the legislative structure of the sample states, attitudes and priorities developed in regard to the hazardous waste problem are translated into legislative initiatives that address the total control issue and specific problems of effective enforcement. Such a "reactive-adaptive" route to criminal law revision is clearly manifested in Maine but in a manner more discretionary than in the other sample states. Maine, with its milder form of state industrialization, followed traditional legislative enactment patterns and the strategic policies of its attorney general's office.

New Jersey's early and flagrant dumping incident, and its heavy industrialization, induced that state to make expedient use of its body of environmental laws carrying criminal penalties. Here, the genesis of criminal law can be traced from the early employment of "common nuisance" laws, to the construction of more problem-specific statutes, to legislative revision in response to obstacles encountered in the course of enforcement.

Maryland and Pennsylvania also put a high priority on hazardous waste legislation and enforcement and displayed upgraded levels of legislative development. Maryland lawmakers carefully evaluated the hazardous waste management problems of the state and as a result created a distinct legislative act apart from its solid waste legislation. Pennsylvania aimed at the sources of problems; with an eye toward the future, it attempts to ensure that management planning is well defined, accounting for waste type and volume generation within the state.

The sample states shared a common bond in that, over time, their state legislators widened the range of criminal definition, proscribing many more improper disposal-related activities as criminal activity; penalties became increasingly severe. These states applied the legally unconventional concept of *strict criminal liability*, rather than the more traditional mens rea requirements, to at least some hazardous waste crime statutes. This was done to broaden the scope of activities covered under these laws and to transfer emphasis from offender intentions to resulting public harm and risks of public harm.

Further aggressive courses of action were taken by Pennsylvania, which drastically lengthened the criminal statutes of limitations on hazardous waste offenses, and by Maryland, which eliminated them. Illegal dumping that may escape discovery for an untold number of years thus remains within the realm of criminal definition and subject to prosecution.

As expressed in interviews with attorneys from these states, the legal thrust of many types of improper handling of hazardous wastes not only became more retributive but tilted toward deterrence of individual prospective offenders. For New Jersey, this plan took the form of sharp penalties against individuals and offending firms that could ultimately result in lengthy prison terms and corporate dissolutions and/or charter forfeitures.

Enforcement Structures

The enforcement structures of all the sample states featured interagency investigative/prosecutorial strike forces. Despite variations in make-up and structural formality, the strike forces were all intended to coordinate civil, criminal, and administrative responses to effectively allocate available resources and by doing so avoid the overlapping of agency efforts.

The following are descriptions of the individual state versions of enforcement at the time of the study with complementary descriptions of characteristics structures as they exist at the time of publication of this edition of *Dangerous Ground* (2015).

Maine. Because of its relatively small volume of hazardous waste crime cases, Maine's interagency task force structure was less formalized than those of the other sample states. But a firm, cooperative effort aimed at the criminal prosecution of hazardous waste offenses linked the Natural Resources Section and the Criminal Section of the Maine Office of the Attorney General with the Maine Department of Environmental Protection and the Maine State Police.

The Natural Resources Section of the attorney general's office maintained legal responsibility (both civil and criminal) for hazardous waste enforcement activities; related prosecutions were handled by its own attorneys. Potential civil and criminal cases requiring court action were directly referred to the Natural Resources Section by the Board of Environmental Protection. Investigations and prosecutions, however, could be carried out by the Natural Resources Section without prior consent from any other state government agency. Investigative support was typically drawn from a cadre of investigators of the attorney general's office and from the state police.

The original decision-making powers regarding the determination of the criminal or civil routes of prosecutions resided with the state's attorney general. If a decision was reached to prosecute criminally, appropriate personnel were briefed by the section chief and contact with the Criminal Section would be made to obtain additional criminal investigative assistance and to facilitate review of documents charging wrongdoing.

At present (2015), the Maine Attorney General's Office maintains independent authority to enforce or prosecute violations of Maine State environmental laws generally, and has specific enforcement authority under statutes governing conservation easements and unfair trade practices. The Maine Attorney General's Office is not authorized to provide legal advice or representation to private parties. The Maine Attorney General's Office continues to be committed to protecting Maine's environment by providing legal advice and representation to the following State environmental and natural resources agencies: the Department of Agriculture, the Department of Conservation, the Department of Environmental Protection, the Department of Inland Fisheries and Wildlife and the Department of Marine Resources

Maryland. Maryland's Hazardous Waste Strike Force was first organized in 1981 and, at the time of the study, was comprised of assistant attorneys general, criminal investigators from the Maryland State Police, and support staff of the Office of Environmental Programs (which later evolved into the state's Department of Environment) of the Maryland Department of Health and Mental Hygiene. The strike force attorneys and investigators, while comprising an integrated and autonomous unit, were housed within the health department building and worked closely with that agency. An additional early member of the task force was the state's Natural Resource Police.

The most distinguishing facet of Maryland's Hazardous Waste Strike Force was that prosecuting attorneys have maintained some responsibility for both the civil and criminal enforcement of hazardous waste statutes, although it later came to concentrate more on criminal investigations and prosecutions. This was in contrast to New Jersey and Pennsylvania, where there was a distinct demarcation of such responsibilities, with the state environmental protection agencies assuming all civil prosecution powers.

While matters of water pollution and general refuse disposal were processed by the attorneys, hazardous waste enforcement became their highest priority. Their civil role had been centered on the review of administrative orders, representation at administrative hearings resulting from appeals of orders and of administrative civil penalty assessments, and the institution of civil actions for injunctive relief and/or civil penalties. Due to an enhanced state emphasis on the criminal enforcement of hazardous waste violations, the most substantial portion of the attorney's time evolved into the direction of criminal investigations and prosecutions throughout the state.

The Maryland Environmental Crimes Unit (ECU) of 2015 includes three Assistant Attorneys General, one civilian investigator with extensive environmental science and investigation backgrounds, and one Maryland State Police trooper assigned as an investigator. Police investigators maintain their normal police qualifications and acquire the training necessary to enable them to fully investigate environmental crimes, including sampling and safety protocols. The Maryland Department of the Environment provides support to the ECU, promoting regular interaction with Department of the Environment's inspectors and other technical experts.

New Jersey.   Sharply rising incidents of indiscriminate hazardous waste dumping in New Jersey, peaking in the early to middle 1970s, led to the emergence of a state-wide investigative/prosecutorial program in 1978. The Toxic Waste Investigation/Prosecution Unit was initiated by the New Jersey Division of Criminal Justice (the criminal enforcement arm of the state attorney general's office) and became the first unit of its kind in the nation. The original modestly staffed unit eventually gave rise to an Interagency Hazardous Waste Strike Force, including additional personnel from the New Jersey State Police, the New Jersey Department of Environmental Protection, the New Jersey Division of Law, the United States Environmental Protection Agency, and the United States Attorney General's Office for the District of New Jersey. A leading role was played by the Division of Criminal Justice, with a deputy attorney general placed in charge of the force.

The Division of Criminal Justice's Toxic Waste Investigative/ Prosecution Unit grew into the Environmental Prosecutions Section of the agency. As a component of the New Jersey Interagency Hazardous Waste Strike Force, the section was responsible for the investigation and prosecution of hazardous waste and water pollution offenses. While county prosecutors' offices could prosecute such cases, many of them were referred to the state's Division of Criminal Justice for investigation and prosecution. The staff of the Environmental Prosecutions Section was comprised of deputy attorneys general, investigators, and support staff.

By 2015, the entity responsible for environmental crimes at the state level was cut back to a unit within the Specialized Crimes Bureau. The unit is now responsible for the investigation and prosecution areas outside of environmental crime including casino and labor prosecutions. The Environmental Crimes Unit is responsible for the investigation and prosecution of violations of the State's water pollution, air pollution, hazardous waste and solid waste laws, as well as traditional crimes that have an impact on public health and safety and the environment

Pennsylvania. Pennsylvania's criminal investigation/prosecution task force, at the time of the original study, was made up of personnel on permanent detached assignment from the state's Office of the Attorney General and Department of Environmental Resources. During the course of the study, the Toxic Waste Investigations/Prosecutions Unit was directed by a deputy attorney general and included one other criminal attorney (who devoted half of his work responsibilities toward hazardous waste crime enforcement), five criminal investigators, and one attorney and five inspectors from the Department of Environmental Resources. The functions of the criminal investigators of the attorney general's office and those of the environmental protection inspectors were quite separate in that the criminal investigators assumed no technical roles (for example, chemical sampling, testing) but only pure investigative responsibilities, while environmental inspectors engaged solely in regulation and technical inspection.

Criminal complaints were received by the task force from state agencies, among other sources. The preliminary review of referred information was generally followed by the decision to pursue the case through a criminal prosecution or to refer it to the Department of Environmental Protection for Civil Action.

At present (2015), the Pennsylvania Office of Attorney General, Environmental Crimes Unit investigates and prosecutes violations of state environmental laws governing the processing, transportation, storage, or disposal of municipal, residual and hazardous waste. Most criminal prosecutions are initiated pursuant to the Solid Waste Management Act, Clean Streams Law, Air Pollution Control Act, Radiation Protection Act or Oil & Gas Act. All Special Agents in the Environmental Crimes Unit were reported as having extensive training in the handling of residual and hazardous waste and are sometimes called upon to assist the Pennsylvania Bureau of Narcotics Investigations with methamphetamine laboratory search warrants. Currently, the Pennsylvania Office of Attorney General does not have original jurisdiction to investigate or prosecute environmental crimes. However, the Office does obtain jurisdiction over an environmental crime by a referral from either a district attorney or a state agency with enforcement duties pursuant to statute.

5

Distribution of Data

Who Is Represented by the Study's Sample?

One might conclude, given the sample structure, that the study over-represents those hazardous waste offenders who are inexperienced or stupid enough to be caught and overlooks those more sophisticated offenders able to elude discovery. However, it is felt that the data represent a substantial proportion of seasoned offenders for several reasons. First, preliminary discussions with sample-state attorney general's liaisons indicated that, based on their experience, many of the offenders they prosecuted demonstrated long records of behavior in violation of regulations, often bordering on criminal actions or, in fact, unlawful behavior. Each liaison characterized his or her regulatory agency as practicing a "cooperative" strategy in regulatory enforcement that would allow such actions to continue until they become too severe to be overlooked or were brought to the attention of the attorney general by other sources (for example, citizen reports, local law enforcement observation).

Interviewees warned that hazardous waste criminal violations are, by and large, *mala prohibita* offenses—acts that are crimes because they are prohibited by the law—and the difference between what is and is not criminally prosecuted is often contingent upon an assessment of seriousness (duration of offenses, amount of waste illegally disposed, dangerousness of chemicals). They also commented that treatment-facility, hauling-firm, and waste-generator offenders are not thought to be one-event offenders, because their profits are based upon frequency of commission and volume of wastes as well as on continuous generator pressures to dispose economically.

These comments support the idea that cooperative regulation gives a sense of legal "immunity" to repeat offenders. In effect, sample-state authorities have been aware of this population of offenders (regulatory and/or criminal) for some time; only recently have criminal investigative/prosecution entities been permitted to assume wide enforcement roles that could threaten the offenders' sense of security.

It is also believed that advances in hazardous waste detection methods played a major role in limiting the number of offenses escaping discovery by authorities. All of the states had been members of the Northeast Hazardous Waste Project since its inception in 1980. This committee was a consortium of state attorney general and environmental protection offices committed to the advancement of hazardous waste crime detection, investigation, and prosecution methods by means of training and interstate information exchange.

The sample is representative of two major categories of offenders. The first comprises those rare, one-event offenders whose unsophisticated and obtrusive actions, due to a lack of experience in such criminal ventures, "beg" detection (i.e., *situational environmental offenders*). The second, much larger, and believed to be truer, component of the offender population are those hazardous waste handlers targeted by enforcement through records of ongoing regulatory violations and spotlighting of criminal arrangements made by treaters and haulers with generators (i.e., *entrepreneurial environmental offenders*).

Occupational Characteristics

The total study sample consisted of 71 cases, 121 individual offenders, and 70 instances where a business firm was charged as a defendant (see table 5.1). The largest category of offending firms in Maine, Maryland, and Pennsylvania was hazardous waste generators (Maine—3 [100 percent of offenders], Maryland—8 [62 percent], Pennsylvania—15 [52 percent]). (see table 5.2). In contrast, the largest offending firm category for New Jersey was TSD facilities (17[68 percent]). Enforcement personnel interviewed attributed the high number of offending TSD facilities located in New Jersey to the growth in volume of the

Table 5.1. Criminal Cases and Offenders Disposed by State.

State	Cases Disposed	OFFENDERS DISPOSED	
		Individuals	Firms
Maine	3	3	3
Maryland	21	27	13
New Jersey	23	61	25
Pennsylvania	24	30	29
TOTAL	71	121	70

Table 5.2. Firms Criminally Charged by State.

State	Generator	Hauler	TSD Facility	TSD Hauler	Landfill	TSD Generator	Total Charged
Maine	3	0	0	0	0	0	3
Maryland	8	1	1	0	2	1	13
New Jersey	1	5	9	8	0	2	25
Pennsylvania	15	9	1	0	4	0	29
TOTAL	27	15	10	9	6	3	70

Note: Encompasses only firms criminally charged as defendants.

state's hazardous waste coupled with an early enforcement emphasis on TSD-type businesses; this early emphasis is one reason that these facilities assumed such a prominent role in New Jersey as the officially identified hazardous waste offender.

Sample results revealed that executives of offending firms that generate, haul, or dispose of hazardous waste are typically influential in furthering the criminality of their professional subordinates. Offenses were generally engineered through the impropriety and endorsement of owners and executive officers of the offending facilities or firms. As can be seen in table 5.3, the number of executive officers charged in the sample exceeded the number charged in each employment-level category.

Organizational Complexity of Offending Firms

By and large, the offending businesses within the sample demonstrated fairly simple organizations—64 percent employed fewer than 50 employees at any one time. The simplicity in organizational structure for generating firms, as well as for hauling firms and TSD facilities, may have contributed to the filtering down of criminal involvement from upper organizational levels.

The prevalence in the sample of small generating firms is thought by those interviewed to be attributable to the relative ease with which authorities can detect the crimes of small-generator offenders and the high success level of their associated prosecutions. Small-firm offenders afford a high visibility of criminal activity and a generally clearer culpability, unlike large-generating firms, which are more apt to dispose illegally, and conveniently, on-site. Interviewees considered it improbable that large generating corporations would resort to forming contractual agreements with outsiders (haulers or treaters) to

Table 5.3. Criminal Case Charging of Firms and Firm Officials.

State	Firm or Official Charged[a]	Firm and Official Not Charged[b]	Total Cases
Maine	3	0	3
Maryland	19	2	21
New Jersey	19	4	23
Pennsylvania	21	3	24
TOTAL	62	9	71

[a] Represents cases in which the firm or a firm official was criminally charged. Officials include the president, vice-president, secretary, treasurer, or owner of the firm.
[b] Represents cases in which only lower-level firm employees or independent operatives were criminally charged.

dispose illegally, thereby protecting themselves from discovery. As is shown later in this book, enforcement's inability to understand these industries' manufacturing procedures unwittingly helped strengthen the protective shield of on-site disposal.

Table 5.3 supplies further insight into the question of individual employee offenders operating independently of their firm.

As can be seen, cases where neither the firm nor any of its officers were charged numbered only 9, or 13 percent of the total cases in which firms were charged.

The majority of these offenders were either non-firm haulers or other "entrepreneurs" who decided to make informal pacts with generators to dispose of their wastes with few questions posed as to their ultimate destination. In Maryland the independent entrepreneur was best exemplified by a construction contractor who, after completing his building labor for a local college, offered to dispose of the school's stored wastes at a nominal fee. In New Jersey, entrepreneur offenders would pose as treaters, accept wastes, and warehouse and abandon them or, in one case, dupe others into buying trucks that, unknown to the buyer, were loaded with wastes.

In only two of these nine cases did middle-management or lower-level employees act criminally with a goal of self-interest. Both were cases where the offenders were middle-management personnel of waste-generating firms whose responsibilities included insuring that hazardous wastes were properly disposed of. The employee in charge of waste disposal for one generating firm conspired with a hazardous waste hauler, falsified manifests, billed the corporation, stored the wastes, and divided the generating corporation's disposal payment. In the second case, the generator employee accepted a bribe from a representative of a TSD facility in return for the employee's discretion in using the treater's services as opposed to those of other qualified vendors.

Waste Sources

These findings on how large industry generators create criminal opportunities by erecting obstacles to successful enforcement help us understand the apparent incongruity of results on sources of illegally disposed wastes. The sources of these wastes reflected some of the preeminent industries of the respective sample states as indicated in table 5.4. However, while most of the illegally disposed wastes were from chemical-producing and petrochemical industries, none of the sample generators fell into these categories.

An overview of the separation of waste sources by states shows that the illegally disposed wastes mirrored some of the dominant industries of the respective regions. For instance, Maine's cases evidenced textile-, wood-, and fishing-industry wastes whereas much of the New Jersey sample's wastes were derived from the chemical-producing and petrochemical industries. Pennsylvania and Maryland samples displayed a significant concentration of cases where primary waste sources were metal electroplating, galvanizing, and other metal treatment processes. Much of these wastes were cyanide-laden sludges from the bottoms of plating baths or spent halogenated solvents used in degreasing processes. In the balance of Pennsylvania's

Table 5.4. Sources of Illegally Disposed Hazardous Waste.

Sources of Hazardous Waste	Number of Cases[a]
Paint-Dye	15
Electroplating/Metal Treatment	14
Petrochemical Industry	11
Chemical Industry	10
Transformer/Capacitor	6
Tank Car Refurbishing	3
Pathological Research	2
Printing	2
Other	11

[a]Represents the presence of the wastes in individual cases. More than one source may appear in a case.

sample cases, it was found that many involved the illegal disposal of petrochemical wastes.

A waste-type source that was unique to the Maryland sample was that of pathological research wastes. These were wastes generated by medical-use industries and are largely comprised of medical specimens and samples. Maryland interviewees reported that because of the wealth of federal institutions and major medical universities in the vicinities of Washington, D. C., and Baltimore, the proper treatment of medical wastes has become a significant problem for Maryland. As a result of the stringent standards Maryland imposes on the treatment of such wastes, those institutions intent upon properly treating the wastes must transport them to out-of-state facilities. This translates into high costs for the generator and an added incentive for illegal disposal.

6

Working the System

In his 1985 study of property offenders and drug addicts, Malin Åkerström observes that adopting any type of crime as a livelihood requires cunning and inventiveness. This is a necessity not only to successfully commit the crimes but also to work the system to one's own criminal advantage. Designing strategies to outwit the justice system is one way to defend a criminal life-style and to demonstrate control.

The study of hazardous waste crime offenders reveals the average offender to be quite imaginative in devising ways to shape the legal environment to his liking. By employing methods of duping environmental inspectors and prosecutors and by establishing partnerships with influential outsiders, hazardous waste offenders were often able to capitalize on flaws in the system to successfully protect their lifestyles.

Manipulating Regulators

The mark of a successful hazardous waste criminal—one who can maintain his criminal life-style for a lengthy duration—is his skill in effectively analyzing the potential threats to his livelihood and his versatility in adapting to these threats. For many TSD-facility operators, the serious game of working the system was played out by eluding the regulatory inspectors by capitalizing on either the inspectors' unfamiliarity with treatment apparatus or their lack of diligence in inspecting thoroughly. Offenders accepted this feature of their lifestyle as a chess game in which they needed to participate or otherwise risk discovery—and often, they won. One owner/president of a New Jersey TSD facility commented: "I'd describe the inspectors as 'slow.' I usually found myself several steps ahead of them, sometimes without trying too hard. Some of the inspectors that were coming to the site, they didn't know what was going on. All they would look at is the pipes. They just asked which way the material went. They weren't really interested in retention time, you know. They asked you but never stayed and observed and took samples."

One TSD-facility employee told authorities how an absence of inspector initiative to examine treatment apparatus thoroughly permitted that facility to continue, unimpeded, to operate criminally for a protracted period. At this facility a clarifier tank had been originally installed to churn wastes in the separation of floatable oil and settleable suspended solids. Skimmer blades at the top of the tank and scraper blades at the bottom were intended to circle and scoop up the materials as they separated from the water. Over time, the scraper blades began to jam, prompting a management decision to slice them down, destroying the tank's ability to treat wastes. However, the rotating upper level blades and the churning wastes were enough to obscure the inspectors' view of the tank's bottom and, thus, to earn passing assessments. As the worker reported, management's boldness grew to the point where the scraper blades were entirely removed, a situation that was found in no way to jeopardize the illegal operation.

Since the same facility functioned beneath the disguise of a waste-oil reclamation center, some inspectors required convincing that the facility indeed was separating oil from wastes. But, once again, detection avoidance entailed little imagination or difficulty of execution. "To take care of the inspectors from the state," said one New Jersey TSD executive officer, "[an employee] would send one of the fellows out to pick up quarts of oil, you know, the kind you put in your car, maybe 10, 20 weight, whatever. [He] would pour them into the clarifier so it had a layer of oil showing that there was oil that was being recovered."

TSD-facility offenders did have to contend with monitoring devices, installed by regulators, that were used to gauge volume and properties of effluents released into local sewer systems to determine compliance with existing discharge standards. The mechanisms were intended to sample effluents randomly but, in reality, offenders found the system seriously flawed and did not hesitate to seize their opportunities to work the system in a new way. A TSD-facility owner/president remarked: "They [the local sewer authority] were pulling grab samples and there was a yellow box there that would click on every 15 minutes or so. So, if you ran your material for approximately 10 minutes, you had 5 minutes to then fill up the area that the test was going to be taken with and [a supervisor] would have [a yard worker] or someone throw chlorine in there so when it was tested it would get a minimal charge." The tests were simply rigged to elicit a false impression of the toxicity of the substances discharged into the sewer.

The simple flushing of effluents for dilution purposes at inspection times was a common method of avoiding detection by regulatory inspectors. Employees serving as "lookouts" were sometimes deployed at TSD facilities with orders to delay entry of visiting regulators. This being achieved, the concomitant task of other employees would be to flush relatively uncontaminated liquid through the facility's plumbing system and processing equipment to alter artificially the chemical properties of the waste to be sampled.

Recognizing Inspection Cycles

Gauging inspector skills in detecting violations and making efforts to counter these skills provides one layer of criminal insulation for the hazardous waste offender. Further insulation is gained if the offender can predict the timing of visits by regulatory inspectors. In fact, the study sample found a disturbing element of regulatory enforcement in the unintentional predictability of inspections. Offenders searching for any means to work the system could easily piece together timing cycles of inspections and alert workers to employ their best detection-avoidance skills at the right moment.

According to one Maryland investigator, the rotating basis upon which Maryland regulatory inspectors operated produced a predictable pattern in that certain facilities were inspected at the same time each month. In two New Jersey sample cases, personnel of an offending treatment facility would be aware of impending inspections and perform makeshift clean-up operations to give the impression of proper functioning. Especially in the beginning of regulatory inspection of waste treatment facilities, inspectors were taken advantage of by facility operators in this way. Some saw this as the natural by-product of investigative naiveté and the adoption of a cooperative enforcement stand. In the words of a New Jersey investigator:

> It was new to everyone and there were inspectors who were naive to a degree. I don't think the inspectors had the proper attitude toward the people they were supposed to be inspecting. Sometimes the inspector would call up the facility and say "Look, I'll be there on Wednesday at ten o'clock." The facility people would have coffee, donuts, and things like that and would clean their act up. The inspector wasn't crooked. He was a kid coming out of college with an environmental science degree, and he was naive.

> Their original attitude was that these people were basically honest and that they were in business to legitimately make more money. Well, most

were in business to make a *lot* of money. If they followed regulations they wouldn't make a huge amount and would start to cut corners. The only way to "nail" them would be to walk in on them blindly.

Co-opting Regulators

Hazardous waste offenders have been known to strengthen their shield against punishment, by trying to bring regulators into the criminal fold. The co-opting of inspection officials is not something new in businesses answerable to regulatory agencies. While the public at large may believe that regulatory agencies operate without consent of the businesses they regulate, there is some historical evidence to the contrary (Hopkins 1979; Clinard and Yeager, 1980). In contrast to the common, two-part legal system of enactment of laws by legislatures and application by courts, both the issuance and enforcement of regulations are responsibilities of regulatory agencies. This leaves the regulatory agency vulnerable to business pressures regarding both legislative and enforcement functions. When such pressure is strong, the regulatory agency's primary mission may be sacrificed (Clinard and Yeager 1980).

Co-option of regulators sometimes involves tempting the officials with promises of generous corporate positions upon resigning from their regulatory positions. Such promises can be quite effective in neutralizing regulatory activities by keeping regulators mindful of how zealous enforcement might affect future career prospects (Clinard and Yeager 1980). The later hiring of the co-opted regulators also holds a clear side benefit for the regulated businessman—he gains a new source of inside information to be used in his battle against violation detection. TSD facilities that engaged in such practices hired building inspectors and law enforcement officers to serve with the companies. In an especially bold undertaking, offenders hired municipal police officers as part-time security guards.

Offenders in the sample were not above resorting to a much less subtle method of co-option—bribery. In three cases bribery was officially charged and appeared, but was not officially charged, in three other cases. In one case, bribes to a building inspector became so financially draining to one TSD facility that the decision to hire the inspector as a full-time employee was based on the belief that paying his salary would be a cost-saving alternative.

The hiring of former state regulatory agency attorneys allowed TSD-facility operators to gain a definite edge in evading state regulations. Facility operators would take full advantage of the former state workers' expertise in the targeting of legal trappings and loopholes. To some regulatory inspectors, the seductive salary rewards were difficult to resist; overtures by the facility heads were made far in advance of job offers to exploit the inspectors' value while they were still state employees. The Maryland assistant attorney general observed:

> There is at least a far correlation of government people going into the industry. It doesn't take all that long for the average inspector to realize he is in a "squat pyramid." There are 500 inspectors, three regional supervisors, and one boss. And probably, if you started as inspector, you'll never make it above the boss level—ever. You might make supervisor, but you're not qualified for the next job up which is head of any agency, and they always look for an engineer or something. And, you're not an engineer because if you were you wouldn't be an inspector. If that's going to happen . . . and if the guy [treater] is being nice to me, I'd better be nice to him because I may apply for the next opening.

Making Connections

Much has been made of the importance of certain outsiders to sustaining the criminal world. In his analysis of the environment of the 'villain fraudster," Levi (1981) describes how such outsiders assume functionally distinct roles and how one individual may fill more than one role. Sparks et al. (1982) explained how ancillary tasks performed by these outsiders can include the furnishing of alibis, critical materials, and the disposition of stolen property—elements that can ensure the success of the central criminal operation.

Just as the fraudster may need to form partnerships with those providing him with a "front," or property thieves may need to do business with "fences," the long-term hazardous waste criminal works hard to populate his world with those furnishing protection from the law. For the hazardous waste handler moving from a legitimate profession to an illegitimate one, he will need to make the right connections to ply his criminal trade unhampered by enforcement.

The average criminal TSD operator does not start out as an especially shrewd corporate offender or a savvy racketeer planning to reap a windfall by means of a criminal career. He is more of a business entrepreneur gone bad. These offenders typically assume great financial risks by entering the hazardous waste treatment business, with its financially demanding technology. Once the TSD operator/offender fully converts his business into a criminal enterprise, he graduates to a more sophisticated criminal stage requiring resourcefulness to sustain his new unlawful life-style. He learns to cultivate a network of outsiders who can help to build a wall between him and those who wish to bring him to justice. "Their crimes become more and more a daily affair to cut corners," said a New Jersey deputy attorney general. "As it became a daily affair, they began to see that there were business contacts out there who could make life easier for them in a criminal sense. It could be the local building inspector who could be bribed, or, better yet, a 'crooked' treatment broker who could lead the 'right' waste generators to the facility. . . . After a while you get to know the ins and outs of the system and how to work it to your best advantage."

Throughout the states studied, the most common outside connections reported by interviewed law enforcement personnel were private laboratory chemists and waste treatment brokers. The private laboratories have the potential, by way of their waste-sample testing responsibilities, to provide an important service to those directing or executing the illegal disposals. In essence, they can supply the stamp of legitimacy in the crucial determination of the hazardous or nonhazardous qualities of the waste in question. As insurance against future offense convictions, the long-term offender will search for a private laboratory that employs dubious ethics in its testing practices. The test results, which "authenticate" the wastes as nonhazardous, can then serve to justify the offender's conduct and help immunize him from successful prosecution.

As a Maryland investigator explained, a number of laboratories in that state have gained the reputation of servicing waste disposers with conveniently liberal test readings: "There are four or five labs in Maryland that if you send the same PCB sample to these labs you'll get four or five varied results. Some have a reputation of much 'lower' results than others. That's the one you want to deal with. . . . It sure gives them a defense—'Here's our lab analysis of the sample. They [the lab] claim it is not hazardous and you guys [the prosecution] are saying it is. We didn't know that. Our lab said it wasn't.—' They get that lab sheet in their hands that says the waste isn't hazardous. That's all you need." Interviewees noted that this informal arrangement perpetuated by unprincipled laboratory operators is a natural profit-growth strategy for these operators. The labs that partake in such conduct promote their reputations for the unethical testing of samples to broaden their base of customers searching for just such improper services.

The more criminally astute offenders use these laboratories as a recruiting ground for the full-time hiring of the more unscrupulous chemists. As a full-time employee of the waste handling facility, these pseudo chemists transmit a sense of legitimacy to potential clients and, in effect, broker the facility's criminal services. "After I would go into the company," said a TSD-facility operator/offender, "I would try to 'sell' the fellow [waste generator] on the company. Then [the facility chemist] would come in and, you know, he would be able to talk openly on anything that had to do with chemicals. They would know they were talking to a 'chemist.' That's how we would get the business. That's why [the facility chemist] got a third of the profits."

Some TSD offenders benefited in other ways by sharing their "criminal space" with facility "chemists." The chemist facade of legitimacy served not only to deceive generators, but also helped convince lower-level TSD employees that their work-site safety was guaranteed. As noted by a Maryland assistant attorney general, this illusion could help trivialize the real danger posed to employees by unsafe work conditions. "One of our terrible concerns was that these people [facility chemists] were incompetent. Even though this guy had a Ph. D. in chemistry, he was frightening. From a safety standpoint, he would permit unbelievable storage problems to exist. It was a horror show. . . . Even as lay persons, workers there should have realized it was a dangerous way to handle these materials. . . . At the trial, it was brought out that some activities that the chemist condoned involved having the employees mix incompatible wastes that were potentially explosive."

Overshadowing the private laboratory chemist as a significant connection, is the hazardous waste broker. Some investigator interviewees noted that, with the passing of time, such brokers have played more critical and unchecked roles in facilitating hazardous waste offenses. The legitimate brokerage function involves contact with generators seeking economically attractive avenues for the proper disposal and treatment of generated wastes. For a prescribed fee, the broker locates hauling firms and/or TSD facilities certified to handle the given wastes and links them with the generators. Unscrupulous brokers will "front" for a host of inexpensive haulers and TSD-facility operators willing to dispose of the generated wastes illegally. The underpricing patterns of such firms produce greater business and enhance the broker's marketability. "It's becoming more and more prevalent," says a New Jersey investigator. "It's profitable. You're handling all the work for the generator and all the work for the hauler. What a way to make money. *The generator pays you, you pay the hauler*, and a lot make deals where you pay me so much and I'll pay you so much. So it's very *profitable*.

And you don't even have to move out of your bedroom, you can do it right from your house. It's all a matter of phone calls."

The broker role as a significant outsider to the offense is growing, in part because of the low visibility of their actions and in part because of an absence of government regulation of the brokerage function. In addition, brokers are exempt from government licensing prohibitions against hazardous waste haulers and TSD operators possessing criminal conviction records. Ex-offenders in hazardous waste crime are thus free to enter this related, potentially lucrative field and take full advantage of their former criminal contacts. "Essentially, if I get convicted of a dumping offense and I want to become a broker there is nothing to stop me," says a New Jersey investigator. . . . All I am is a broker. I don't 'handle' hazardous wastes, I don't sign manifests, and I don't need to be permitted by the Department of Environmental Protection. And the law basically says anyone convicted of a crime cannot apply or be licensed to be engaged in any hazardous waste business in New Jersey. And technically [brokering] is not a hazardous waste business."

So, the hazardous waste offender has worked the system to a point where developing criminal opportunities by making the right connections has been replaced, at least in the case of the hazardous waste offender/broker, by the creation of self-serving positions exempt from environmental law.

The Hazardous Waste Offender: A Criminal Innovator

Focusing on the life-style of the hazardous waste criminal permits an unusual glimpse of how this type of offender manages to reap huge profits by capitalizing on a flawed regulatory system and constructing a countervailing web of personal acquaintances and business contacts. Be it duping regulators, co-opting them, or cultivating a network of "helpful" chemists and brokers, the long-term hazardous waste offender displays a talent for effectively evaluating the vulnerabilities of both his legal and business environments in his quest to preserve his criminal career. It is evident that the dumping of hazardous waste—and getting away with it—is a skill that must be mastered.

The skillful hazardous waste offender learns to reduce risks whenever possible. To accomplish this, he need not have a commanding knowledge of legitimate treatment/disposal techniques, but he does need to assess accurately how much of this technical information is understood by regulators and criminal law enforcers. He is thereby able to finesse his way into being perceived as a legitimate operator for long periods.

As a true exploiter, he educates himself in the professional drawbacks of the regulator's job as part of an effort to lure regulators into the criminal world. He pinpoints the inspection routines of "slow" regulators, forms illegal bonds with those who test the waste, and may even go as far as bankrolling building inspectors. And, if all else fails, and he is arrested and convicted, he can console himself with the realization that he may someday be resurrected as a "treatment broker" with the latitude once again to make the most of inadequate regulatory laws and defective regulator enforcement.

As a criminal innovator, the hazardous waste criminal does not restrict his opportunity-seeking to the associations forced upon him in the legal and business worlds. Truly to reduce his risk of punishment, he cannot afford to be so myopic. His innovations can—and often do—extend beyond these worlds to the actual physical environment in which he operates.

7

Physical Surroundings and Detection Avoidance

The criminal resourcefulness of the long-term hazardous waste offender does not end with his development of connections to the "right" outsiders. It is also displayed in his manner of viewing everyday surroundings and events in terms of their criminal, or crime-covering, potential. In this way, he is much like other types of career criminals (like drag distributors and robbers) described by Åkerström (1989) and Loveland (1976). Far from being a passive offender, making the grade as a career hazardous waste offender can require a good deal of thoughtful planning, as noted by one New Jersey law enforcer: "The guy who is trying to make a living from illegal dumping has to be on his toes to make sure we aren't on to him and at the same time make a profit. It can be a lot of work for him. . . . 'Creative' may sound like an odd word to use to describe them, but in a way they are. I think that some of them could have become very successful noncriminal businessmen if they wanted to."

Capitalizing on Opportunities to Avoid Detection

The professional hazardous waste offender faces a number of major challenges in his criminal career, not the least of which is the challenge to conceal satisfactorily his criminal acts from the eyes of the general public as well as from the eyes of law enforcement. From spotting the chinks in the armor of regulatory enforcement to distinguishing the opportunities presented by his natural surroundings, the accomplished hazardous waste offender is an expert at shaping circumstances to maximize his odds for escaping discovery. Unlike those who undertake other types of clandestine crimes, such as thieves, the hazardous waste offender not only seeks ways to elude detection of his actions as he commits the offense but also must hide what he has left behind—the object of his crime—to avoid the tracing back of the wastes by government technicians.

Just as the hazardous waste offender becomes a workmanlike student of legal and business vulnerabilities, he also must be willing to read the detection-avoidance possibilities inherent in his region's natural resources. The wily offender is aware that what may be seen as recreational treasure to the average citizen can also be the key to complete insulation from criminal detection.

Being criminally learned, here, also means being attuned to how the same topographical features deemed undesirable by the general population can be desirable for the purposes of the illegal disposer. A blighted landscape, pockmarked with boreholes descending to what were once underground mines, can be the site of a bonanza for the sharp-sighted criminal disposer hunting for a reliable means of camouflage.

The lay of the land, from a detection-avoidance perspective, will help the offender decide where, when, and how the offenses should be committed. An examination of each sample state's distinctive physical characteristics regarding opportunities for low-visibility criminal acts gives us some clues to the actors most likely to become criminal offenders and where they are apt to commit the offenses. In Maine, Maryland, and Pennsylvania, offending generators discharged into sewers and/or bodies of water. In New Jersey, criminal treaters typically disposed on-site or in abutting waterways. Locations where waste-filled drums were abandoned or where wastes where released onto grounds in remote areas varied widely in the states of Maryland and New Jersey. They ranged from beneath overpasses, in wooded areas, on desolate land near railroad tracks and farmlands, and rundown urban areas. Although the perpetrators proved themselves genuine opportunists, they could not match the criminal ingenuity of other offenders in Maryland and Pennsylvania who either set up their own pseudo landfills for illegal dumping or took full advantage of the detection-avoidance potential offered by abandoned mines.

Landfill crime cases in Maryland and Pennsylvania grew out of unauthorized landfills that, over time, gained a level of unofficial public acceptance because of an absence of regulatory enforcement attention. These landfills were unlicensed and usually originated by enterprising landowners. In one Maryland case, a makeshift landfill had been in operation for several decades and under numerous owners until the hazardous waste acceptances led to criminal charges and subsequent landfill shutdown. Regulatory violations were sometimes issued by state agencies, prior to the imposition of criminal charges, but these warnings were often ignored. Occasionally, the operator would ease into the landfill business as a direct by-product of what was, or what appeared to be, a legitimately run enterprise (for example, a metal reclamation firm). Operations would then be gradually expanded to accept and landfill hazardous wastes from customers of the legitimate business.

Pennsylvania's underground labyrinth of mines became a haven for case-sample offenders; six of Pennsylvania's "nonconsensual abandonment/release" commissions occurred at or near active or inactive mining areas. In one active mine, toxic fumes from released wastes wafted in from a vent, causing a potentially explosive condition—the igniting of coal dust. The deadly risk posed to mine workers present at the time precipitated the mine's evacuation. In what was Pennsylvania's most serious hazardous waste crime case, massive amounts of wastes—over three million gallons in approximately a two-year period—were released into an abandoned mine borehole and eventually flowed through the subterranean channels into the Susquehanna River.

Offenders' Occupations in Relation to Disposal Methods

The interstate comparison of offenders who discharged wastes into sewers and those who discharged into nearby bodies of water (such as streams and creeks) revealed an occupational division between generator offenders in Maine, Maryland, and Pennsylvania, and TSD and TSD/hauler offenders in New Jersey (see table 7.1). In 12 of the 13 instances in Maine, Maryland, and Pennsylvania, where either sewer discharges or discharges into bodies of water were committed, the offenders turned out to be generators. By contrast, six of seven of New Jersey's sewer-discharge and water-discharge cases were conducted by treaters or treater/haulers. Ten of the total 11 sewer-discharge cases, for all states, were committed on-site at either the generator or TSD facility. All of the total nine water discharge commissions were committed by generators of TSD–TSD/hauling facilities that abutted or were in close proximity to a waterway that would permit easy run-off or direct flushing, usually through an underground piping system or hosing apparatus.

The New Jersey landfill commissions of offense were markedly different in terms of criminal responsibility as well as in commission structure. Those criminally charged were offenders responsible for either transporting, treating, or generating the substances that were eventually disposed at landfills. Neither landfills nor landfill operators were charged in connection with any of the commissions. This does not necessarily suggest that landfill operators were not in fact criminally involved, but rather could reflect enforcement difficulties in establishing knowledge of violations and complicity.

Table 7.1. Methods of Improper Disposal/Storage by State.[a]

State	Stockpiled	Consensual Abandon/Release on Private Prop.[b]	Nonconsensual Abandon/Release	Landfill Disposal	Sewer Discharge	Discharge into Body of Water	Other
Maine	0	1	0	0	0	3	0
Maryland	11	11	2	3	4	2	2
New Jersey	9	3	8	6	5	2	2
Pennsylvania	4	6	10	4	2	2	3
Total	24	21	20	13	11	9	7

[a]Represents the case presence of the above types of offense commission. More than one type may appear within a case.
[b]Represents cases where some agreement was made between the generator and the property owners as to the disposal of the waste.

Cooperative Arrangements among Firms

If he is especially opportunistic, the hazardous waste offender will not only recognize the exploitability of the immediate natural environment, but will also identify other offenders in the industry who can "lease" their man-made facilities as detection-avoidance insurance.

Cooperation among offenders to benefit from ideal plant locations was found in certain TSD facilities in the New Jersey sample. Although the TSD industry in that state was discovered to be quite competitive and virtually devoid of anything resembling a genuine cartel, criminal cases were encountered where interfacility cooperation in networks was developed. TSD facility operators seeking ways to reduce their chances of detection would often search for other facilities willing to take the risk of accepting and disposing of their high volumes of wastes. These cases were characterized by company officials searching for expedient waste removal outlets prompted by regulatory pressure and storage space scarcity.

In the diagram, TSD_3 represents the "savior facility"—that facility willing to assume the most substantial legal risk of accepting and unlawfully disposing of the materials. This facility would also possess a location or complex construction that is markedly better isolated from surveillance than that of the transferring facilities. It thus capitalizes on capabilities for successful avoidance. (Other similar group-crime offences are described in Chapter 9.)

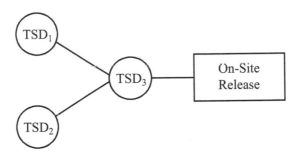

The savior facility arrangement is a simple example of interfirm agreement that merely scratches the surface of the more complex, interfirm waste-oil cases explained in detail in chapter 9. The arrangement, also, only hints at the more intricate *intrafirm* relationships common to criminal TSD workplaces that form the bedrock of a well-defined, quasi-bureaucratic criminal apprenticeship system.

8

Creating a Criminal Maturation System

The way thieves learn their illegal profession has frequently been referred to as a tutelage process in which novices are "trained" by their more seasoned companions. Although this description may be an oversimplification, it does set the stage for understanding a similar type of relationship found in the TSD-facility offender workplace. The relationship transcends the simple, teacher-student relationship. It is characterized, by turns, by trust, antagonism, and solicitation. Most important, it serves as the lifeblood of long-lived criminal TSD-facility enterprises.

The Track to Criminality

The world of the hazardous waste offender operates on two tracks, leading to the transformation of legitimate treatment/disposal businesses into criminal businesses. As can be seen in figure 8.1, these tracks are both incremental but are fueled by different incentives.

The upper-stratum offender—the operator/owner—is motivated by profits from illegal relaxation of acceptance standards for incoming hazardous waste. This is done gradually and becomes increasingly flagrant as regulatory enforcement weakens and as operating costs and business competition grow.

While the upper-stratum offender turns to crime to increase profits, the lower-stratum offender—the yard worker, the truck driver—disposes illegally as a means to sustain employment. The lower-stratum offender's initiation into hazardous waste crime is, in short, an appraisal process conducted by organizational supervisors, where performance in carrying out marginally criminal directives decides how overt future criminal directives will become.

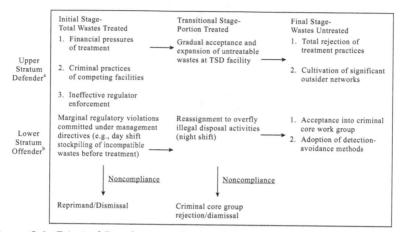

Figure 8.1. Criminal Development Stages of the Hazardous Waste Offender.
[a]Includes TSD owners, operators, and managers
[b]Includes TSD truck drivers and yard workers

The Upper–Stratum Offender: Architect of Hazardous Waste Offenses

Though the cooperative efforts of upper- and lower-stratum offenders often end in the successful execution of hazardous waste crime, the characteristics of each group are unique, as are their tracks into criminality.

TSD-facility personnel backgrounds reflect the workplace dichotomy of upper and lower socioeconomic levels. TSD management offenders were rarely found to have criminal backgrounds. This was explained by interviewees as a by-product of the relatively short history of the connotation of improper hazardous waste disposal as crime. These offenders did, however, have long histories of regulatory violations, and were seen by respondents as persistently walking the line between regulatory and criminal violations, occasionally testing the boundaries of law enforcement with overtly criminal dumping.

The TSD operator's descent into crime typically is prompted by the progressive relaxation of the facility's waste-acceptance standards for those forms of wastes the facility is ill-equipped to treat. Some capacity to treat hazardous waste existed in most of the sampled New Jersey facilities, but treatment equipment was generally so inadequate that many forms of hazardous waste could not be treated safely.

The Lower–Stratum Offender

Unlike their superiors' backgrounds, those of lower-level TSD-facility employees commonly include past criminal offenses. Enforcement personnel interviewed saw this as a reflection of a blue collar–white collar bifurcation, in which truck drivers and yard workers operate in a social climate more tolerant of certain criminal indiscretions than that of the executive officer. Because ex-offenders are seen by the TSD bosses as potentially more compliant with criminal directives, criminal records are sometimes used as a selection criterion. This criterion is often coupled with that of technical naivete regarding hazardous waste danger and the criminality of improper disposal.

The lower-level offender possesses scant technical knowledge of the dangerous properties of illegally disposed wastes and typically does not understand the level of self-harm inherent in his improper handling of these wastes. Occasionally, supervisors will make specious efforts to educate handlers in an attempt to present a facade of safety consciousness. One lower-level employee, a Maryland hauling firm yard worker, described his supervisor's efforts as perfunctory at best: "[The supervisor] brought me a book. I forget what it was called, but it's simple and easy ways to dispose of chemicals. We never followed that per se. We never got around to it. He's too busy to get rid of the rest of the stuff like that. But, first year high school chemistry only takes you so far."

Operators sometimes find that their selection formula for criminal complicity is not foolproof. In these cases they have to venture beyond a singular reliance on the criminal backgrounds and technical naivete of subordinates to promote systematic TSD-workplace criminality. The key for developing such criminality is the creation and nurturing of a normative work environment supporting illegal hazardous waste disposal.

Moving Up the Ladder

The criminal conversion process of the lower-level employee is central to the entrenchment of criminal norms at the TSD-facility workplace. Usually, this process begins innocently enough with worker participation in normal day-shift activities. But select workers may then quickly be ordered to complete marginally criminal assignments like the lateral stacking of incompatible wastes. Acquiescing in such directives signals the transition to the next criminal conversion stage. Here, the worker is reassigned to those activities constituting the chief source of the workplace's illegal disposal. This usually means exclusive contact with the facility's "core group" of veteran criminal disposers. It also means confinement to a low-activity shift to preserve insulation of criminal actions from other workers.

To counteract any qualms regarding the propriety of dumping, the novice core group member is likely to be persuaded by long-standing members that his actions are not unlawful. Any resistance to criminal directives at this juncture ends in the abrupt termination of employment. The final conversion stages include not only the commission of overt offenses but also an active participation in detection avoidance, which marks the completion of the TSD subordinate's criminal conversion process from novice employee, to reluctant coconspirator, to willing criminal participant. Although the entrance points of upper- and lower-level TSD-facility offenders are different, their criminal tracks merge at a point where overt criminal acts are not only encouraged but necessary for continued employment.

The complete criminal conversion process was best illustrated in the documentation of a New Jersey case where a yard worker, of a TSD facility adjacent to a waterway, commenced his employment with responsibilities of mixing wastes with solutions to produce usable by-products. After several promotions, he found himself laboring near the water's edge, secluded from the rest of the facility, connecting waste-filled tanker trucks to a grounded hose. Coworkers and supervisors alike maintained the hose was linked to underground holding tanks. The worker's confidence in this explanation was shaken after he witnessed wastes surfacing in the abutting waterway. The worker at first questioned the legitimacy of the activities, but became satisfied that the procedures were part of the normative structure. When reality eventually set in, as reported by the worker, he had become a fairly long-standing participant in the criminal activities and decided it was prudent to remain within the group and practice a self-imposed silence with other, newer employees at the facility.

These developments were not confined to TSD facilities. Similar situations were reported by lower-level employees at firms in other sample states. These cases also displayed a criminal transformation that frequently ended in an acceptance of the criminal disposal as being unobjectionable. In a major generating facility, wastes from metal-treatment solution vats were commonly discharged into floor drains. As these acts had become a mainstay procedure for years, those lower-level employees ordered to release vat valves expressed shock when prosecution ensued.

However, as one employee put it, the persistent use of the discharge practices did not entirely obscure their wrongful character: "When I first went to work there, I would shut the valve. After I was there a while, I learned it was sort of—it seemed to be standard practice not to. I'd have to say I 'winked' at it."

Covert Reward Systems at the TSD Workplace

The preceding description of the development of hazardous waste offenders allows for a fuller understanding of lawful and unlawful work relationships in the TSD workplace and of how these relationships constitute the misuse of a legitimate business to promote environmental crime. The resultant crimes, regrettably, characterize the industry as a whole in the 1970s and 1980s. Prospective TSD operators wishing to enter the industry needed only minimal technical skills and a willingness to comply with weak licensing standards to become legally licensed. Because it was a fledgling technical industry in an atmosphere of desperate generator and public demand for legitimate treatment outlets, it attracted inexperienced entrepreneurial types prone to placing faith in their own abilities and, later, when that became impractical, to evading treatment-process regulators.

These operators became the initiators of a vertically structured system in which they bend the rules of legitimate TSD operations to cultivate covert reward systems for themselves. Although these covert reward systems are not always available to all who work in the criminal TSD operation—the introduction of special screening mechanisms take care of that—they do make up part of the total rewards system that joins formal legal rewards (wages, salaries, commissions) with illegal rewards (returns from illegal dumping). The work relationships in criminal TSD facilities fall into the category of what Mars (1982) would call "covert institutions": "it is the regular presence of total reward systems and of the networks of work-based social relationships through which total rewards are deferentially allocated to individuals by what I term *individual contracts* that are the 'covert institutions' of occupational life" (11).

The criminal TSD facility functions by adopting certain deviant organizational goals (for example, the improper stacking of drums of incompatible wastes), and by adopting deviant means to achieve certain legitimate organizational goals (for example, the disposal of hazardous wastes into municipal sewer systems). The operative goals of such a business, as pointed out by Schelling (1970), is usually determined by the organization's "dominant coalition," who collectively control organizational resources so that they may be selectively distributed to those chosen as the executors of the crimes. The "dominant coalition," or "criminal core group," of the TSD facility is the fulcrum of the criminal operations of the agency, and as such represents the final stage of the lower-level offender's initiation into the criminal dumper's world.

An important finding for the study of hazardous waste crime in the TSD work place is that two parallel goals/means systems can be operating simultaneously as day-to-day TSD work activities move along. It is the "shadow" goals/means system that is most dangerous for public health, for it is this structure that sets the tone for the commission of the most serious offenses. It sets into motion the steps needed to be taken for the future illegal dumper to prove his mettle and grooms him for his imminent criminal career. And it is not uncommon for these criminal maturation systems to operate unbeknown to those workers outside of the criminal core group. A TSD-facility yard workers said:

> The guys that did the dumping with me sort of hung out with me—outside of work as well as on the job. . . . The other yard workers were sometimes told to do some things that would be considered minor infractions. They were never ordered by our supervisor to do the actual dumping. I don't think they knew that we weren't treating the wastes. They figured they knew what we were doing and were doing it on the "up and up." Anyway, they were too concerned about their own jobs. . . . Most of them never became part of our group. I guess the boss felt they didn't have the knack for our type of work, or else he didn't trust them. . . . We all worked at the same place, but we were really in two different worlds with us taking home a lot more in pay.

The sad reality is that existing criminal systems become so firmly entrenched in the workplace that they prove difficult to dismantle. Unless prosecutors are successful in shutting down operations, the prosecution of core group individuals and their managers can ultimately be fruitless. "If one of the guys who dumps gets into trouble with the law," the yard worker added, "somebody else will be picked or hired to take his place. . . . Even if one of the supervisors gets caught, there will be someone else at work or they have enough connections with people outside of work to bringing in the 'right' person to get the job done. . . . Unless the place is shut down, somebody will find a way—maybe a little different way—to get the job done."

For the hazardous waste crime enforcement community, nullifying the illegal actions of individual criminal managers may, indeed, amount to a shallow enforcement gesture. Once firmly established, TSD-facility workplace subcultures seemingly could easily survive without the services of those managers removed from the criminal mainstream by prosecution.

9

Hazardous Waste Crime as Organized Crime

As has been shown, the average hazardous waste offender has more in common with the Ivan Boesky ideal that with that of Don Corleone. The average dumper appears to be an entrepreneur who starts out by running a safe and legal business. But harsh competition, lax enforcement, and ample opportunities to go astray tempt our would-be tycoon into becoming a real-life criminal.

Yet questions still remain: What role, if any, does syndicate crime play in advancing the criminal careers of these offenders? Are certain areas of hazardous waste generation and treatment industries more vulnerable to syndicate crime invasion than others? If so, what makes them so vulnerable?

Where does hazardous waste crime fall on the continuum of organized crime—from simple group crime operations to incidents implicating the participation of syndicate crime associates? Although they are not as beholden to syndicate crime organizations as other writers would have us believe, some hazardous waste criminals are not above relying on aid from syndicate families when deemed necessary. Those disposal offenses that represent the far end of the organized crime continuum (syndicate crime connections) are localized within one sample state, New Jersey, and appear to be thriving in one specialized industry—the waste oil industry.

Defining Organized Crime

The four-state study took a continuum approach to the subject of organized crime espoused by such criminal justice scholars as Smith (1980) and Hagan (1983) (see chapter 3).

Sampled criminal cases were analyzed through documented case examples of (1) law enforcement identification of offenders as members of known syndicate crime families; (2) attempts to influence criminal enforcement and regulatory officials through bribery or other corruption; (3) attempts to form monopolizing customer allocation systems similar to the property rights system existing in the solid waste industry in some parts of the country; (4) the use of violence or threats of violence against person or property; (5) unlawful restrictions upon potential newcomers to the hazardous waste disposal transporting/ treatment industry by trade associations or unions; and (6) any evidence of a hierarchical structure of offenders. Case file data were, once again, supplemented by more interpretive information gained in interviews with state law enforcement officials.

Organized but Not Syndicate

In the sample, hazardous waste offenses committed as acts of a formal, criminal monolith were rare. The generator offenses were criminally organized only on the most fundamental level; organization usually took the form of simple criminal conspiracies. These criminal arrangements often were ongoing but were primarily designed for illegal profit without the typical hallmarks of traditional syndicate racketeering (for example, threats of violence or corruption of officials). In the New Jersey TSD industry, however, the level of criminal organization was much more sophisticated and exhibited some of these syndicate properties.

In New Jersey, syndicate crime family associates were found to enter the TSD industry by organizing favor systems for failing entrepreneurs, but these associates far from dominated the study sample. Their presence proved to be an infrequent occurrence compared to the more familiar TSD offender as imprudent business entrepreneur.

The usual form of organized hazardous waste criminal behavior in the sample was a loosely knit, independent criminal unit based on the triadic nature of the legitimate hazardous waste disposal processing cycle (generator, hauler, and treater). Early criminal offenses grew from simple, individualized offenses, such as midnight dumping, that were eventually prone to failure as a result of enforcement advancements, and rose to a point where small detection-avoidance enterprises were formed.

Overall, these criminal units were not as large or as centralized as traditional syndicate crime but did manage to improvise a degree of criminal sophistication in the workplace structure. The units sometimes sprouted into networks of TSD-facility personnel and outsiders like *unethical disposal/treatment brokers and private laboratory chemists,* whose help could build an aura of legitimacy around criminal activities.

Group Crime

It is fundamental to organized crime analysis to recognize the degree to which offenders within the sample function in concert with other offenders to commit offenses, such as the operation of a simple conspiracy. Research delving into this area is at least as illuminating as testing the waters of a higher level of syndicate crime: it supplies insight into group crime characteristics of the offenders' professions (generator, hauler, treater), but also sheds light upon how these group offenders elicit the help of others operating outside the illegal disposal realm.

Table 9.1 presents an incremental picture of sample cases where (1) criminal conspiracies were charged; (2) criminal conspiracies were not charged, but case file data indicated that two or more offenders had acted in concert to commit the offense(s) and were charged for the offense(s); and (3) cases where two or more offenders worked in concert in the commission of the offense(s) but only one was criminally charged.

The table leads us to the inescapable conclusion that forms of group crime are present in most of the sample cases if the definition of "group" is not limited by the artificial criterion of official criminal charging. This is particularly so for the states of Maine, Maryland, and Pennsylvania, where the criminal charging of conspiracies did not seem to be a part of the criminal charging style of enforcement agencies in those states.

The major difference between sample states was that in New Jersey, conspiracies occurring *within* firms were generally committed by employees of TSD facilities. In other states, these single-firm group crime episodes took place in waste-generating companies. Across states,

Table 9.1. Multiple-Participant Criminal Incidents and Charging Practices by State.

State	Multiple Offenders/ Conspiracy Charged	Multiple Offenders/ Conspiracy Not Charged	One Offender Charged/Multiple Participants Reported	Total Criminal Incidents
Maine	0	0	3	3
Maryland	1	7	11	19
New Jersey	13	5	1	19
Pennsylvania	3	8	8	19
Total	17	20	23	60

Note: Criminal incidents involving multiple participants are also referred to as "group crime" cases.

many of the group crime offenders, who were employed within the business enterprises, were offenders working in cooperation in an official business activity, with the group effort being directed by an employee at a middle-management level or above. Lower-level employees, in each of the cases, took on the responsibility of the actual execution of offense (for example, abandonment, land release, sewer discharge).

The behavior patterns existing in cases where group criminal activities were interfirm were characterized by complexities not common to the intrafirm cases and deserve a more thorough analysis by type. Type 1 interfirm group crime is an example that is described by authors such as Mustokoff (1981).

This diagram shows the conventional triad wherein criminal agreements can be made between generator, hauler, and TSD-facility operator, or any combination of them, to illegally dispose of the wastes at a savings to the generator and an increased profit to the hauler or to the TSD operator. Naturally, a variation of this triad is where the generator pays the full amount for proper treatment/disposal

Type 1.

and is defrauded. The third segment of the triad diagram has been altered from simple TSD facilities to reflect landfills as the final destination most frequently present in Pennsylvania and Maryland cases. Typically, for those states, haulers either formed bonds with landfill operators to insure waste acceptance, surreptitiously disposed in landfills without operators' authorization, or dispensed on the hauler's land in makeshift landfills unapproved by the states.

Type 2 interfirm group crime involves a group activity initiated by "cooperative generators."

Type 2.
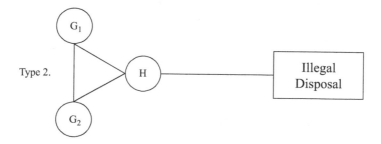

This relationship highlights the significance of the role played by informal information exchange between generators to update their awareness of the most "economical" disposal methods. In this mode, Generator 1 forms an initial criminal alliance with the hauler in which the hauler collects the wastes and, shortly thereafter, disposes it unlawfully. Generator 2, in a product enterprise similar to that of Generator 1, searches for an identical relationship and, through business inquiries, is apprised by Generator 1 of the arrangement that can be achieved with the hauler. Both generators thus engage in an ongoing relationship, with a sense of legitimacy to their involvement emanating from the knowledge that neither is alone in misconduct.

Cooperative behavior, in the commission of offenses, was also evidenced among certain TSD facilities in New Jersey. Although the TSD industry was found to be quite competitive and ran counter to any cartel structure, criminal cases were discovered where interfacility communication networks were utilized in a search for facilities willing to accept high volumes of waste from other facilities.

Syndicate Crime Presence: State Results

Within the sampled criminal cases from Maine, Maryland, and Pennsylvania, there were no instances of offenders or associates of offenders identified as members of known, highly organized syndicate crime families. Of the 13 environmental crime investigators and prosecutors interviewed within those states, none saw any evidence that highly organized syndicate crime was associated with hazardous waste crime in their states.

While many of the offending waste haulers in the Maryland and Pennsylvania sample cases had been employed as solid waste haulers, the question of a customer allocation system of hazardous waste hauling firms became somewhat academic. Not only did interviewees deny the existence of such cartels in the hazardous waste disposal industries of these two states, but the hauling firms and TSD facilities were not part of any hazardous waste hauling/treatment labor unions or trade associations. Both transporters and treaters in these states were seen by enforcers interviewed as operating fairly independently within a highly competitive market.

The criminal cases examined in Maine, Maryland, and Pennsylvania exhibited no instances of threats of violence against those in the hazardous waste disposal industries, or to those applying for licensing, in an attempt to impose membership restrictions within those industries.

69

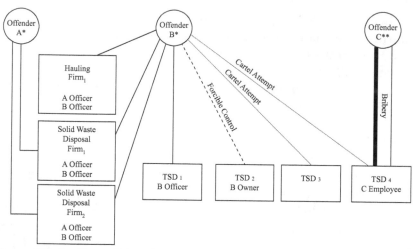

Figure 9.2. Syndicate Crime Associate Links to Waste Hauling Firms and TSD Facilities in New Jersey.
* Reported association with syndicate family 1.
**Reported association with syndicate family 2.

There were no cases where offenders in these states attempted to gain "immunity through corruption." No briberies or attempted briberies were charged within the three states nor were any such allegations made within the cases.

The organized crime analysis results for New Jersey proved to be different from the results in the three other sample states. At least one of three organized crime associates appeared in each of three New Jersey cases, eliciting charges for the illegal disposal of hazardous wastes. Figure 9.2 presents the connections between sample offenders with associations to identified syndicate crime families and solid and hazardous waste hauling firms as well as with TSD facilities.

By the early 1970s, the individual identified in the figure as offender B had been successful in developing a garbage disposal firm (Solid Waste Disposal Firm$_2$) and in wresting a lucrative garbage disposal contract from its previous contractor. Offender A was, at that time, the "unlucky" owner of the disposal firm that lost the contract (Solid Waste Disposal Firm$_1$). Shortly after, these two solid waste disposal firms merged and offenders A and B became executive officers and major stockholders. Offenders A and B were found to have close associations with syndicate crime families in New York and New Jersey. Offender B was linked with highly placed mobsters in a syndicate involved in loansharking and the carting industry. This crime family supplied offender B with financial support to the tune of over \$1 million so that he could pursue his business operations. It was also known that offender B was helped by syndicate crime members in sealing garbage contracts in exchange for kickbacks.

In time, offender B widened his business and criminal interests to include hazardous waste hauling firms and TSD facilities. He master-minded a profitable criminal operation that called for the transportation of hazardous wastes from a New York hazardous waste storage facil-ity and the later abandonment of these wastes near some New Jersey railroad property. As a representative of the parent firm subsidizing TSD_2, offender B eventually became part-owner and executive officer of the treatment facility. This came on the heels of offender B's threats against TSD_2's former owner to coerce him to relinquish facility con-trol. Predictably, offender B allowed conditions at his newly acquired business to deteriorate and the property flowed over with a jungle of stored drums filled with toxic chemicals. As an ostensible response to demands by the state environmental agency to reduce drum volume, offender B concocted a scheme to shift drums from their unlawful accumulation at TSD_2, to TSD_1.

As an ideal example of the hazardous waste criminal as opportunist, offender B also plied his trade by recruiting owners of other TSD facili-ties (TSD_3 and TSD_4) into an illegal facility cartel. He tried to strong-arm the owners to enter into a property rights system modeled after the solid waste industry. Offender B even prodded the two owners to enlist other TSD owners into the cartel. The envisioned customer allocation system never got off the ground. Much to offender B's disappointment, his grand plan fell victim to the TSD operators' overriding attention to the implementation of the then new manifest tracking system and the bearing it would have on regulatory enforcement.

A similarly ill-fated cartel creation attempt was later initiated by offender B involving the operators of TSD_4. This failed effort was brought about through contact between offender B and a TSD_4 sales representative (offender C) who was identified as having close links with a second syndicate family. Acting as a representative of syndicate fam-ily 2, offender C interceded and effectively blocked the cartel attempt.

Focus on New Jersey

As mentioned earlier, the organized crime analysis results for New Jersey proved to be different from the results in the other three sample states. In 3 of the 23 New Jersey cases reviewed, officials of charged facilities were identified as being associates of a traditional, highly organized criminal syndicate. The case examples position them at the extreme end of the organized crime continuum. The data indicated that those offenders with syndicate associations are more likely than the average hazardous waste offender in the sample to have criminal records. Also, the criminal cases within which they were involved represented high-volume illegal waste disposal activities over protracted periods of time. These facts acknowledged, it is also necessary to note that an analysis of all New Jersey sample cases reveals that the majority of the cases (20 of 23) displayed no involvement by associates of syndicated crime families (in the form of law enforcement identifications, bribes, threats of violence).

In regard to any crossover impact from syndicate crime influences in New Jersey's solid waste industry, investigators interviewed confirmed that the early involvement of operatives in the solid waste industry did play a part in introducing known syndicate associations into the hazardous waste industry. But these same interviewees noted that the several efforts to create a customer allocation system modeled after the solid waste industry met with a predictable demise. They concurred that the development of hazardous waste customer allocation systems failed, and with it any syndicate crime control that would have followed. This failure was due to some noteworthy properties of illegal hazardous waste disposal that could not apply to the solid waste industry. In the words of a New Jersey investigator:

> The key to the entire solid waste industry is you control the haulers, the "stops," and you control the place where the garbage has to be taken.... You can't take a garbage truck and just dump it on the street or in the woods because garbage is contingent upon volume and you have to have a place to put it. So, the garbage industry has organized crime all over it. On the other hand, the organized crime involvement in the hazardous waste industry can't control "Corporate America." They're not going to control the people that generate the material.... On the illegitimate end . . . all you need is access to a sewer, the woods, or whatever. Organized crime cannot control the fields, woods, or access to sewers. So you're not controlling the disposal site; it can be anywhere. When it's anywhere, there are opportunities for anyone to do it. All you need is a truck and the ability to move barrels.

Interviewees thus illustrated that the expected crossover of solid waste operatives had taken place, especially during the late 1960s and early 1970s, accompanied by some of the same syndicate crime associations that prevailed in that industry. However, it soon became apparent that the degree to which nonsyndicate crime offenders could easily dispose of hazardous waste rendered this industry an unadaptable arena for a syndicate crime-controlled system. Several syndicate crime associates were, indeed, able to position themselves as officers and part-owners of individual treatment facilities, as was depicted in the study sample, but this fell far short of fulfilling any grander syndicate crime goal of orchestrating a complete control system within the hazardous waste industry.

Intrastate Offender Networks

As a part of the organized crime continuum analysis, criminal and noncriminal association networks were studied with a special eye toward (1) the types of relationships that unite these networks and (2) the variety of roles played by the network actors.

The New Jersey case sample displayed two networks of associations interlinking several key offenders from the New Jersey case sample. Rather than being an interweaving network directly linking each actor with every other actor, figure 9.3 explains this network as a progressive one, with indirect linkages dominant between actors.

The network flow commences with actors 1 and 2 as, respectively, an officer and an employee of TSD_1 during the early 1970s. The "promotion" of actor 2 to officer of TSD_2 connects to the nucleus of the first phase of the total network (TSD_2) from which actor 3 and the officer of TSD_2 (actor 4) widen their business base to include H1 and TSD_4.

The second network is composed of the interconnections of offenders 5 and 6 and their roles as executive officers/owners of five facilities/firms. Offender 6 provides the pivotal link in network 2 as he functions as an executive officer of TSD_7 along with offender 5; but offender 6 also has an important business interest in two other offending hauling firms. Chronologically, these connections conclude with the criminal prosecution of these actors in the early 1980s.

At two points, unsuccessful attempts were made by members of network 1 to consume the business interests of network 2. One of these acts was an effort by owners of TSD_1 to buy out TSD_6, and the other was a more coercive attempt by offender 4 upon offender 5 to draft TSD_7 into a never consummated TSD cartel.

As described by a New Jersey investigator, the actors of both networks represent the "elite offenders" of early offense cases, some of whom crossed over from the solid waste industry into snowballing business

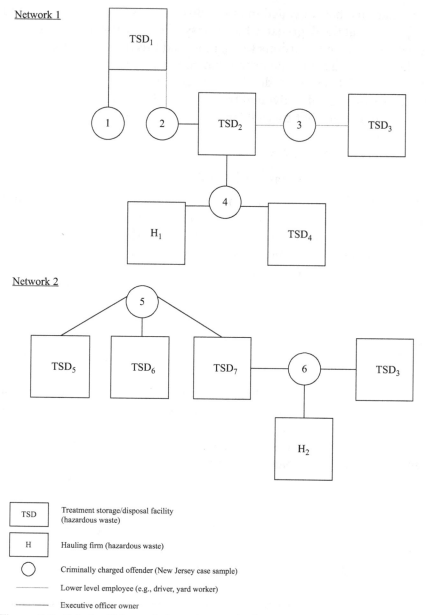

Network 1

Network 2

TSD	Treatment storage/disposal facility (hazardous waste)
H	Hauling firm (hazardous waste)
◯	Criminally charged offender (New Jersey case sample)
———	Lower level employee (e.g., driver, yard worker)
———	Executive officer owner

Figure 9.3. Criminal Network Association of Select New Jersey Offenders.

interests in hazardous waste TSD facilities and hauling firms. The relationships represented in the diagram are the most explicit ones and do not reflect some of these actors' more peripheral connections to hazardous waste crime in New Jersey. Their influential nature as key network actors in the New Jersey case sample is reinforced when one considers that 23 of the 61 individuals and 14 of the 25 corporations charged were charged as part of cases involving these actors of networks 1 and 2.

Interstate Offender Networks and the Waste Oil Industry

Although in the original study strong evidence of syndicate crime influence was sparse, one specialized area of the hazardous crime world that does warrant further investigation is the interstate waste oil–hazardous waste connection. A common thread weaving through the cases of illegal, interstate hazardous waste offenses proved to be the disposal and/or treatment of waste oil and the mixing of hazardous wastes with waste oil. Syndicate crime connections to the waste oil industry have been reported by sample-state investigators; the follow-up study indicated a growing concern in a number of states that these types of offenses will surface more frequently.

Figure 9.4 provides a basic overview of the process by which waste oil can be recycled and the critical junctures at which the mixing of waste oil and hazardous wastes would take place. Plainly, commingling can occur at any of three major transferral points from the moment the "scavenger" waste oil hauler accepts the used oil from the waste oil

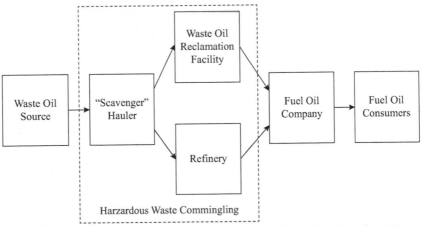

Figure 9.4. Waste Oil Processing Stages and Points of Possible Hazardous Waste Commingling.

source (for example, gasoline filling stations, auto mechanic shops) to the stage at which the supposed recycled oil is burned as heating fuel.

An elaboration of this simple representation magnifies the importance of the crossing of state boundaries for these types of offenders. During the time of the original study, New Jersey and Maine regulated waste oil as a hazardous waste. That is, all manifest tracking systems and restrictions on the methods of legal disposal applied to waste oil as it would to any other type of waste. For Maryland and Pennsylvania, during the period of the original study, hazardous waste disposal restrictions were not applicable to waste oil and, in effect, made these states havens for the importation of waste oil laden with hazardous waste—purely because of varying standards of definition.

The general dynamics of such offenses are outlined in Figure 9.5 which introduces what has been described as common criminal implementation devices.

The operators of the TSD/hauling firm accept both hazardous waste and waste oil from outside sources, mix the substances, and conclude arrangements to transfer the mixture to State 2, where waste oil is not regulated as hazardous waste. In this manner, the operators of the TSD/hauling firm profit by selling the contaminated waste oil to a reclamation facility in liberally regulated State 2 and thereby avoid regulations for the storage and sale of waste oil in State 1. The operators of the waste oil reclamation facility in State 2 may decide to sell the wastes as heating oil within their state or elect to return the waste to State 1 for sale under its newly defined status as waste oil, free from manifest restrictions imposed by State 1. A Pennsylvania investigator explained how his home state plays a part in such circumstances: "What we found

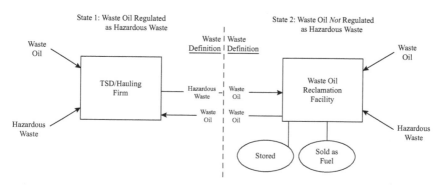

Figure 9.5. Interstate Relations in the Commission of Hazardous Waste—Waste Oil Offenses

is that there is an effort going on where people are transporting waste oil from New Jersey into Pennsylvania via hazardous waste manifests. And, once it hits Pennsylvania it pretty much drops off the books, at least off the New Jersey books. Then it is being transported back into New Jersey on a 'bill of lading' or on a manifest but not listed as a hazardous waste. So it's a good way to hide a lot of solvents."

The difference in definition can be subject to even greater exploitation, as evidenced by a related Maryland incident in which a hauler discovered some previously untapped strategies for profit. After accepting a load of hazardous wastes with waste oil content, and having no particular destination in mind, the hauler was contacted by managers at a facility who offered to resell it as waste oil. The hauler's position became an economically enviable one as he set into motion subsequent criminal acts that are representative of waste oil-related offenses. A Maryland assistant attorney general commented:

> The transporter was getting paid at both ends [generator and reclamation facility] for this stuff and never did anything to it. . . . Then comes a company from Pennsylvania, a transporter, who takes it off [the facility's] hands to take it to Pennsylvania. Of course originally it was manifested as a hazardous waste but now all of a sudden, once it gets to the third party, it has "magically" been transformed to waste oil. So, there is no further tracking or manifesting of it and up in Pennsylvania everyone is pretending it's waste oil. . . . All the tracking along the way is lost and what is worse, all of the environmental controls that are to apply to hazardous waste are gone.

Utility of Results

The results of the analysis of organized crime in the hazardous waste treatment industry are valuable for crime enforcers as well as for the general public. The most far-reaching value is that the results disqualify some previously held notions regarding the hazardous waste offender. Although syndicate crime's presence has been felt in certain aspects of hazardous waste crime, the present discoveries refute claims that syndicate crime has succeeded in totally controlling TSD industries in the sample states. Moreover, syndicate crime's actual role—as benefactors to financially strapped TSD operators, has been clarified, as well as how and why they were, at least up to this point, unable to gain a foothold as monopolizers.

As set forth by Reuter et al. (1983), certain aspects of the hazardous waste industry would render it vulnerable to being monopolized—fixed location of customers, service delivery, low-skill workers. But several other characteristics of the industry have seemingly had the effect of narrowing the chances that a cartel system would become a reality. The two main factors here are (1) the absence of a strong union or trade association to operate as the disciplinary tool for a cartel and (2) the inability of any entity to control individualized occurrences of unlawful disposal of hazardous wastes, especially among potential customers (in other words, generators).

As Reuter explains in his report on racketeers as cartel organizers (1985), because the union furnishes an ideal front of legitimacy for cartel enforcement, it most effectively fills the need of racketeers to coerce facilities/firms into complying with cartel structures. Allegiance paid to cartel mandates comes to be viewed more as socially acceptable loyalty to union rules; noncompliers may be confronted with situations such as union-worker picketing of their customers or union grievance-committee hearings serving as levers for cartel compliance. Such events are not commonplace in the present study's four-state sample simply because hazardous waste associations or unions were virtually nonexistent.

An even more critical hurdle to cartel creation is that total control of industry criminality and its profits cannot be as reasonably attained in the hazardous waste industry via the securing of customer "stops." This has less to do with the service provided by the industry than with the physical state of the wastes involved. The liquid or sludge form permits the hazardous waste generator, or other independent hazardous waste offenders, wider latitude than that allowed in the solid waste industry to dispose illegally without contact with haulers or facility operators. For the solid waste industry, the bulk properties of the waste make unobtrusive disposal of it without cooperation from disposal firms impossible. On the other hand, as pointed out by law enforcer interviews, hazardous waste generators are privy to alternatives other than contracting the disposal firms; hazardous waste can be easily and expeditiously disposed, undetected, and through independent actions. In effect then, total control of the "stops" is circumvented by the broadened scope of criminal opportunities inherent in the hazardous waste industry, which allows a side-stepping of formal contractual agreements.

In a 1986 work on hazardous waste crime, Szasz attempts to explain the role of syndicate crime, so far, in the TSD industry. He contends that generators may be "powerless" to choose disposers because of the existence of a syndicate-controlled cartel of disposers. As we now know, syndicate crime control of the TSD industry has not come close to the

Hazardous Waste Crime as Organized Crime

proportions of control of solid waste industries. The real danger of misinformation on the characteristics of the hazardous waste offender is that it can serve to relieve some of the burden of responsibility from a major category of hazardous waste offenders: hazardous waste generators. It is not hard to imagine that generator offenders would like nothing better than for attention to be diverted from their criminal behavior to a search for a criminal monolith within the TSD industry.

We have seen from empirical evidence that to understand the makings of the hazardous waste criminal we must suspend any preoccupation with suspected syndicate domination. Instead, we should concentrate on the occupational demands and temptations within the relevant legitimate industries. The form and volume of hazardous waste crime is preordained by the criminal opportunities open to the offender within his profession. Rather then being the product of syndicate crime family undertakings, the crimes are outgrowths of opportunities such as (1) seclusion provided by the topography of specific regions, (2) the ability to recruit employees willing to dispose illegally, (3) the availability of criminal assistance networks, and (4) gaps in effective enforcement.

10

Investigation Methods/
Prosecution Obstacles

In determining what is effective in the criminal justice processing of hazardous waste crime cases, two of the most important factors are the ease with which investigators can detect the presence of the offenses, and the courtroom pressures and obstacles encountered by the prosecutors in the latter stages of a case. This chapter describes the most common manifestations of these factors and how they affect the potential for ultimate success or failure of criminal enforcement efforts.

Means of Discovery

A feature of investigations examined for this study is the means by which hazardous waste crimes come to the attention of law enforcement authorities—in effect, the official beginning point of a hazardous waste criminal case.

In 62 of 71 cases, it was possible to identify means of law enforcement discovery, 23 of which were citizen complaints either to regulatory officials or directly to law enforcement authorities. In cases where the citizens reported to local authorities (municipal police departments, municipal fire departments) or regulatory agencies (state environmental protection agencies) the complaints were eventually relayed to attorney generals' offices. In most of these cases the reporting citizens were neighbors of firms where the substances were being transported, stored, or disposed. The most common occurrences that fostered suspicion and prompted neighbors to report were the actual viewing of stored drums, the detection of unusual odors, or the observation of extraordinary activities. In one Maryland case, a change in dumping and filling operations at an unauthorized landfill led to neighbor response. Neighbors saw lights from bulldozer headlamps and heard the noise of dumping operations between 2 AM and 4 AM. This unusual activity, not noticed by neighbors for the 15 years that the landfill was in operation, led to the opening of the criminal investigation.

In several of the citizen-reported cases, the individuals lodging complaints were business competitors of the targeted violating firms. In one of these cases the proprietors of a solid waste disposal firm were bold enough to confirm their suspicions about illegal hazardous waste disposal by a hauler/landfill operator by conducting their own aerial surveillance of the landfill.

The use of competitive operators as original complainants and sources was articulated as being of high value by some of the investigators interviewed. One Maryland investigator described how law enforcement can capitalize on competition within the hazardous waste disposal industry to aid in offense discovery: "Some of your best sources of information are competitors in the industry. Usually they're always willing to 'give up' something on one of their competitors: 'I'd never do this but so and so would.' And then you go to the other guy and find that he does that and you charge him, but he says, 'Well, what about so and so?' Then you may go back to the guy who gave you information in the first place and he's doing something. You get him later. Everyone will roll over on each other generally." This arrangement, however, is not without its drawbacks, as explained by a second investigator. Information may be anonymously provided by investigative targets themselves, or directly provided in law enforcement interviews, as a subterfuge in hopes of deflecting enforcement efforts elsewhere. The second investigator noted occasional law enforcement eagerness to accept this "competitor" information without reasonable reflection.

In one Maine case, the criminal activity was brought to the attention of criminal justice authorities through reports by employees of a neighboring business. The illegal release of anhydrous ammonia into Portland Harbor by an offending fish company was discovered by the employees of a nearby lobster pound after approximately 5,000 lobsters died within a few days.

The next most common source of discovery within the sample, numbering 14, was state regulatory field inspections/document reviews. These included cases that were initiated via routine regulatory examination of records and manifests. In this latter process, the presence of fictitious hauler-manifest numbers or periodic reports listing unauthorized haulers as transporting hazardous wastes sometimes became the deciding factor in earmarking information for referral to the agency. This review procedure was seen by some investigative interviewers as a rich form of proactive investigation. Said one Maryland investigator: "The manifest review from a criminal investigator's viewpoint is needed. You can see trends. You can see one particular driver pick up a load in Maryland and deliver to Ohio. The only trouble is, it's a 12-hour drive and he's done three loads to Ohio in a single day. Something's the matter here."

The next highest concentration of means of offense discovery—11 cases—was through the actions of local law enforcement or local regulator personnel. These were cases in which municipal police, fire, or other local regulator officers observed hazardous waste criminal activities during the course of their normal investigative or monitoring responsibilities. The majority of these cases (7) initiated by local officials took place in New Jersey. The events that precipitated the official's curiosity ranged from early-morning motor vehicle activity at disposal sites, burning wastes, the discovery of abandoned drums, and, in one instance, the release of waste through the rear spigot of a moving tank truck.

Employees of the offending firms proved to be the source of offense discovery in 10 cases. These instances were evenly divided between cases that began as a result of information received by former employees and those derived from information received from employees still employed by the offending firm. The employees reporting offenses were found to fit any one of three categories: personnel (1) who had been ordered by job supervisors to engage in improper hazardous waste disposal, (2) who had not participated in the actual criminal act but had witnessed such acts and complained to management to little avail, and (3) who had simply witnessed the illegal activities.

Accidents were the source of discovery for four of the criminal cases. Two involved explosions at landfills; the others were a highway waste spill caused by the improper vehicle-loading of wastes and a chemical burning of a sanitation worker.

Postdiscovery Sources

Employees of the offending firms were found to be valuable postdiscovery information sources. In 43 of 71 sample cases, either an ex-employee or those employed at the time of criminal investigation became sources of information on the identities of the perpetrators and the methods of perpetration. In some instances, these individuals' contributions were so important that, according to one interviewed investigator, "there would simply be no case without their assistance."

The majority of these cases (26) were instances in which the employees offering information were still employed during the investigation itself. The most common conditions of these cases involved questioning lower-level employees (yard works, drivers) after observation, usually by the enforcement agency, of their committing of offenses. In five of the cases, lower-level treatment facility employees were granted legal immunity in exchange for cooperative information on offense commissions. In some cases, these lower-level employees were confronted with photographic evidence of their illegal activities as a means to elicit their cooperation against those ordering or supervising illicit acts.

Although instances did occur where employees voluntarily reported they were ordered by superiors to participate in illegal activities, these voluntary reportings were rare. Two cases evolved from anonymous telephone callers who were later found to be employees of the offending firms. The internal pressures that would dissuade those employees who might entertain the idea of reporting firm violations are concisely reported by a deputy attorney general in Pennsylvania: "We traditionally get a much lower level of cooperation from employees who are still employed. Not necessarily because they might implicate themselves (that can be done by an ex-employee as well), but because (a) they just don't want to talk to you because they're afraid they'll lose their jobs or (b) they know they might get their company into a jam and in a long-term way they'll lose their jobs. That is, the company may decide to relocate or be forced to close down. So, present employees tend to be of much lower value."

The practice of utilizing former employees who had witnessed or been ordered to commit offenses was reflected in 13 of Pennsylvania's 24 cases. Some of those willing to provide information were ex-workers who had previously reported improper activities to higher firm authorities and had been ignored, while others were disgruntled workers who believed that they had been unfairly treated by their employers. In one case, the employee, a primary information source, remarked that he had quit his position after experiencing a bad conscience regarding his role in committing the offense. As a Maryland investigator described it, "their conscience might bother them or they may have a gripe against their employer; they may have been 'screwed over' once or twice. They feel it [informing] is the best way at getting back at their employer."

Surveillance and Investigative Methods

The sampled criminal case files and investigator/prosecutor interviews revealed a variety of surveillance/investigative techniques that were particularly helpful in the effective prosecution of cases, some of which appeared unique to hazardous waste offenses. Traditional stationary- and moving-vehicle surveillance methods were utilized especially where information indicated that at targeted facilities, specified waste-hauling-firm vehicles were to dispose of or off-load hazardous wastes illegally. Investigators carefully observed the physical characteristics of vehicles and their movements upon entrance to and exit from enclosed areas to determine if the vehicles had discharged their loads. The most typical observation noted was bouncing motions of exiting vehicles, which would noticeably contrast with their relatively stable condition upon entrance. In a representative Maryland case, officials trailed a landfill operator's vehicle from a known hazardous waste generator and used this before-and-after observational technique to ascertain that the waste had been off-loaded. This surveillance directly preceded the execution of a search warrant on the landfill.

Long-range photography appeared to be a particularly useful surveillance method in New Jersey cases that involved treatment facilities and transfer stations that abutted major waterways. Suspected illegal discharges into these waterways were confirmed by investigators who set up surveillance sites on nearby bridges and/or on land across from the waterways. In these cases, long-range photographs often served the dual purpose of furnishing enough evidence to support probable cause for search warrants and to elicit testimony from lower-level employees photographed in the act of illegal disposal.

The safety from exposure that treatment facility walls provide was nullified, to a degree, by the use of aerial surveillance. The most extensive use of such surveillance occurred in a New Jersey case where numerous overflights revealed that a treatment facility, purported to be neutralizing hazardous wastes in large tanks, was not operating its treatment apparatus at all. Helicopter observation detected trees and shrubbery growing in the uncovered treatment tanks.

Interviews also indicated that small-plane and helicopter surveillance could be instrumental in obtaining evidence of other criminal violations at TSD facilities, landfills, waterways, and fields. Examples of this type of evidence included stacked drums, burned patches of grass and vegetation, discoloration in waterways, and heat-sensitive land zones detected by infrared photography.

Noteworthy investigative strategies, apart from surveillance, included undercover investigations, sting operations, document inspections, and the tracing of drum identification markings. In the cases where agents assumed undercover identities, the information obtained proved to be highly productive in that it affirmatively established not only the criminality of offender actions but allowed greater insights into the criminal relationships between employees within the offending firms. In one Maryland case, the undercover agent impersonated a buyer of empty, 55-gallon drums who intended to transform the drums into "piggyback" stoves. The investigator was able to sample the remnants of wastes within the drums to confirm their toxicity. In several other cases, investigators posed as novice haulers. In one such New Jersey case, the investigator formed a bond with a drum recycler under investigation who explained to the agent the intricacies of disposing illegally. The drum recycler also guided the investigator to the recycler's remote dumping sites and suggested an arrangement whereby, in the event of enforcement discovery, the recycler would accept legal responsibility for criminal activities if the agent would pay his legal fees.

In instances where drums were found abandoned in secluded areas, the markings on such drums were pivotal to the identification of the parties criminally responsible. Investigators were able to remove any paint or other substances applied by offenders in an attempt to obliterate identifying markings. Drums could then be traced to drum manufacturers or chemical manufacturers and then to generators. This being accomplished, determinations could then be made as to any agreements generators had made with hauling firms and the terms of those agreements. By noting the type and color of drums plus surrounding materials found at crime scenes, investigators traced responsibility back to a generator-offender in New Jersey. (Pressure-treated wood surrounding the abandoned drums was matched to materials found at the generator's site.)

Where drums were not used to contain illegally released or discharged hazardous wastes, as in several Pennsylvania and Maryland cases, investigators traced the wastes to their sources by comparing the analyzed content of wastes sampled at the disposal sites with sample tests on the wastes of suspected generators.

As a means of verification of illegal discharge and the amount of discharge, comparison analyses of firm records and the amount and types of chemicals found on-site during investigations sometimes proved valuable. The benefit of such analyses was most effectively illustrated in Maine, after flame retardants were allegedly discharged by a generator into a nearby waterway. As part of the ensuing investigation, detectives analyzed bills paid by the generator for purchase of the chemicals to be used in the treatment of textile products. This data, combined with subsequent examination of related invoices and files, indicated that the generator should logically have had a much higher volume of the chemical than was actually found at the time of the investigation. Though this information did not in itself confirm the illegal discharge of chemicals, it proved meaningful in highlighting the unlikelihood that an enormous amount of substances could be properly utilized in the given time frame.

Dye testing was particularly useful in Maryland, New Jersey, and Pennsylvania for tracing the sources of discharge in sewers or waterways. Here, dyes were poured into suspected outlets for offenders' discharges, such as storm drains and pipe systems; the color of resultant discharges was matched with discharges at the source. Investigative techniques like the tracing to points of origin of markings on abandoned drums and the physical properties of disposed wastes were of dual value in that they helped to discern criminal responsibility and also supplied corroborative evidence in the actual prosecution of the cases.

Genesis of Surveillance and Investigative Methods

The combined data gleaned from criminal case material and investigator interviews indicate that surveillance and investigative techniques and, more important, the focus of these efforts have evolved through several stages since the early years of hazardous waste regulatory enforcement. This evolution was necessitated, in large part, by the evolutionary process manifest in the commission of offenses, which, in turn, might possibly be in response to earlier enforcement actions. As explained by New Jersey interviewees, investigative procedures used in hazardous waste crime cases have had to adapt, since the mid-1970s, to ever-changing conditions.

Interviewed investigators in Maryland, Pennsylvania, and New Jersey expressed the belief that increased enforcement had persuaded offenders to modify early commission methods and adopt methods that decreased the risk of detection. Enforcement crackdowns on abandonments and illegal landfill disposals were seen by investigators as playing an integral role in the transformation of commission methods. According to one Pennsylvania investigator, offenders, like those who released waste into Pennsylvania's abandoned mines, may not have foreseen the possibility of eventual discovery: "Who is going to suspect or think that when they dispose 300 feet underground that it's ever going to surface anywhere? You don't realize that all these mines are connected to underground streams and eventually they will surface either in a river or an outfall someplace."

Interviewees noted that as the enforcement of abandonments and disposals in remote areas became more prevalent and effective, generator offenders relied increasingly on on-site discharges and haulers chose to dispose in enclosed areas (such as abandoned warehouses). Consequently, investigators were compelled to revise their methods of enforcement. In the words of a New Jersey investigator:

> It got increasingly difficult to detect illegal dumping. Maybe in the beginning, these people were a little bolder because they figured no one was out there really looking at them. Then later you needed some luck to crack a case; you needed someone "inside." You needed an informant because they wouldn't do it in broad daylight. For those outfits blowing stuff off into a sewer line, normally they would drive a big tanker into a garage and close the doors behind them and hook up the tanker to a manhole inside the garage. So, unless you had information, there was no way of knowing the stuff was going in.

A reflection on offense commission trends over time naturally kindles speculation on the future. Interviewed investigators and prosecutors in New Jersey and Pennsylvania believe that legislation mandating generator responsibility for insuring proper treatment of hazardous wastes, plus the aggressive enforcement of such laws, dissuaded many generators from contracting with haulers and treaters known to be disreputable. The interviewees, projecting on the characteristics of future hazardous waste criminal commissions, warned of a possible upsurge in on-site generator offenses in an attempt to afford further isolation of criminal activity. Also, some investigators have theorized that, as redirected enforcement methods meet with greater success in uncovering offense commissions in such enclosed areas, offenders may opt to take advantage of inadequacies in interstate regulation and interstate enforcement coordination, which, in turn, could lead to a rise in interstate offenses.

Public and Corporate Pressures

Interview results described how the prosecutors of hazardous waste crime are often exposed to the alternating pressures of public demands to accelerate criminal prosecutions and corporate demands to abandon them. Public demands stem from the public fear of harm from hazardous waste crime sites, corporate demands from the fear of ruined reputations as a result of criminal prosecution.

In one Pennsylvania case, in which hundreds of thousands of gallons of hazardous wastes were dumped into a landfill, local residents took to the streets to protest what they considered the inexperience of prosecutors for the case. On the other hand, the Maryland attorney general's office experienced intense pressure to withdraw from the prosecution of a waste-generating corporation that was the second-largest employer in its county. Maintaining that the offenses were accidental, the firm's president publicly threatened to terminate operations in Maryland in response to any criminal prosecutions. After the firm's conviction, he followed through by relocating the operations to a nearby state, and concluded his retaliation with a scathing newspaper report campaign accusing the state government of Maryland of being antibusiness and cautioning other businesses against locating there.

In addition to the pressures of public outcry and business-community opposition, environmental issues other than those posed by hazardous waste sometimes arise as obstacles to prosecution. This was exemplified in Pennsylvania, where a district magistrate at a preliminary hearing dismissed charges against those accused of illegally disposing hazardous wastes at a stone quarry. The magistrate openly admitted that the charges were being dismissed to persuade the state environmental protection agency to address more serious problems existing in the district. The attorney general's office concluded that the dismissal was made because of the magistrate's connection with a citizen's group that was at the time protesting the local settlement of a recycling facility and the state environmental agency's involvement in the matter.

Evidentiary Obstacles

Obstacles to prosecution encountered in the pursuit of evidence of criminal activity arose when investigators allegedly trespassed on disposal sites and when investigative attempts to document exact dates of offense commissions were challenged.

In several trials, defense attorneys attempted to suppress evidence obtained in cases where wastes were disposed on privately owned "open-land" property where "no trespassing" signs were absent. During a Maryland trial, more than 50 charges were eventually dropped by the prosecution because of a lack of sufficient evidence that wastes were disposed on the dates specified. Here, prosecutors were forced to rely on record documentation and employee witnesses to prosecute other charges successfully. In a Pennsylvania case, evidence obtained in a landfill excavation 16 months prior to the trial was deemed inadmissible by the superior court judge. Evidence that the prosecutor referred to as the "centerpiece" of his case was ruled inadmissible because it was judged that the attorney general's office had not presented sufficient reason for its search and the warrant did not specify when the evidence was disposed on the premises. The prosecution was forced to resort to using source information from haulers and neighbors.

In some cases, the technical nature of determining the level of danger or risk posed by disposed wastes, to the satisfaction of judge and jury, prompted both prosecuting and defense attorneys to employ the services of expert witnesses. Prosecutors found it prudent to retain expert toxicologists to explain the potential effects of illegally disposed substances. Expert advice from EPA representatives was used to help determine if accused offenders understood and followed accepted industrial practices for treatment. Thus, on occasion, the courtroom became a battleground of experts, with visual-aid presentations of complicated chemical and scientific evidence and information on state and federal regulations. Interviewed prosecutors reported that their limited resources often placed them at a disadvantage.

Technical assistance appeared to be of greatest value to prosecutors in criminal cases where the offenses were committed as part of specific industrial processes (for example, electroplating, degreasing). "Charges involved things that you can't prove in court and can't even investigate without a significant degree of technical support and technical expertise," said a Maryland assistant attorney general. "That's just the nature of the beast. Hazardous waste is complex and it becomes more complex when you are dealing with industrial operations and corporate operations. Those will always be complex and, indeed, will get more complex because to the extent that someone is deliberately violating the law, they'll use their own sophistication to mask it."

The use of technical expertise in the courtroom has proven to benefit the prosecution in some unexpected ways. Maryland's charging of water pollution offenses in conjunction with hazardous waste offenses serves as an example. Here, not only must the wastes be judged hazardous by prescribed regulatory criteria, but typically toxicologists, biologists, and fish pathologists will serve as state witnesses to certify to what extent the wastes can be classified as water pollutants. The advantage here is that the experts' testimonies, to support the additional charges, will help convey the gravity of the offenses to the jurors and lend greater credibility to the state's position.

A recurrent cause of some distress to interviewed prosecutors, pertaining to the gathering of evidence, was the past insensitivity on the part of environmental agency inspectors to aspects of criminal justice processes, and the implications of that insensitivity for successful prosecutions of hazardous waste crime cases. While respondents generally acknowledged that gains have been made as a result of inspectors' exposure to recent investigative-training programs, they also believe that improvement was still necessary in several areas. The area most commonly referred to was the collection and recording of source information, especially with regard to the conducting of interviews of offending-corporation personnel. Flaws not only encompassed deficiencies in interviewing skills but also the failure to appreciate the constitutional rights of those being questioned. It was felt that the upgrading of such investigative skills through education would lessen the distortion of information collected and the chances that some evidence would be judged inadmissible at trial.

Regulation Concerns

In the sampled cases, criminal prosecutions were periodically stymied when it was discovered that local regulations had been inconsistent with state regulations. This was most common in municipal regulations of sewer-disposal. Prosecutors found in one sewer-disposal case that the local sewage authority had granted a special authorization to a TSD facility, exempting it from normal restrictions and leading to a judicial dismissal of criminal charges. One New Jersey deputy attorney general interviewed added that some municipal sewage authorities did maintain authorization listings of types of waste discharge that were more specific and less comprehensive than state regulations; this sometimes led to legal limitations for prosecutors.

One Maryland assistant attorney general concisely described the typical situation wherein local versus state control over regulation is the ultimate issue. "An overriding area of regulation is one that the state has and that is to control against the unlawful disposal of hazardous waste. It so happens that the methods of sanitary sewer disposal are also regulated by the municipalities. Well, maybe things come to a head there. They may say this is their area of domain and we say the state regulates hazardous waste disposal—period."

Respondents were firm in their opinions on why municipalities' sewer-disposal regulations may be more liberal than those imposed by the state. The prevailing view was that for a mayor or municipal authority to impose liberal sewer-disposal regulations would translate into a signal to businesses that a relocation to the municipality would be accompanied by a desirable measure of freedom in waste discharge. A Maryland assistant attorney general remarked: "They say, 'Well, *this* is a nice city to be in. I'd like to set up my company in this city.' It improves the employment market. The company moves here, hires people—it's good for the city. It's not that the city is interested in just violating the environment per se. It's that it presents a more positive business climate if you have lax regulations. . . . These are matters where our enforcement philosophy is quite different than the city's."

The variable nature of regulations over time was a concern of interviewed prosecutors—a concern borne out, to a degree, within the criminal cases. The most common concern was the long-term variability of state regulations on hazardous waste treatment/disposal. Some offenders voiced objections during criminal prosecutions that because of changes in regulatory edicts it was easy to "unwittingly" commit crimes. In one episode, the presiding judge dismissed charges on the grounds that there had not been sufficient notification by the state environmental protection agency that the accused were in violation of regulations. Several interviewees articulated a certain degree of empathy toward the plight of treaters who may unintentionally violate.

Manifest-System Deficiencies

Some interviewed prosecutors also suggested that inadequacies in state manifest systems, intended to track hazardous wastes "from cradle to grave," have done much to hinder effective detection and prosecution of offenders. One of the most frequent complaints submitted by interviewees had to do with the apparent breakdown of the manifest system when the wastes are destined to be disposed/treated in a state other than that of the generator. Under such conditions, unscrupulous haulers were said to take advantage of a lack of interstate coordination to dispose illegally in the receiving state without ever entering the state's manifest system.

Interviewees also cited loopholes that exist even when the manifest system is utilized within the state of generation. The most sobering example is the success with which one New Jersey offender was able to create the impression of adhering to manifest rules when, in fact, he was violating them. In this case, proper initial procedures were followed in that the waste generator forwarded a copy of the waste manifest to the state environmental protection agency. As the next step, however, the hauler was supposed to deliver the wastes to the identified facility, which in turn was to send confirmation of receipt to the environmental protection agency. Instead, the hauler forged the signature of the facility on the manifest, sent it to the environmental protection agency and released the wastes in a wooded area.

One interviewed prosecutor's recommendation for how to close the loophole is simply to require that generators alert the treatment facility to expect the wastes by sending them a copy of the manifest. A suggestion by another prosecutor to improve the manifest system and to help document methods of disposal was to substitute certificates of destruction or neutralization for simple waste receipts.

11

Discussion of Results

Summary

The study's results have permitted us to answer the questions associated with a variety of areas of inquiry. We found that occupational characteristics varied according to state, with New Jersey displaying more TSD-facility offenders and the other three states more generators. Frequently executives and owners of the firms/facilities were criminally charged, indicating management participation in or approval of offenses. When lower-level personnel were charged with offenses, these were committed for the benefit of the corporation and to ensure continued employment.

Methods of commission of offenses were often found, initially, to take the form of stockpiling; when lack of storage space created pressure, they became more overt. These methods were determined by the availability and types of natural, secluded outlets in each state, and by each state's brand and effectiveness of enforcement. While few offenders had criminal backgrounds and few entered the field with preconceived notions to violate, a double-strata system was developed in many TSD facilities to support criminal careers.

For the most part, offenders were "organized," but not in the syndicate crime sense. In fact, syndicate crime's existence in New Jersey TSD facilities was short-lived and had little industry impact. Any interstate offense networks were based on criminal opportunism in nearby "legal haven" states.

Enforcement response in the sample predictably varied through time and between states. Prosecutorial selectivity and experience, and state-law emphasis, played roles in determining how the offender was officially defined.

This is a quick synopsis of major results in a purely descriptive form geared to prescribed research queries. It is a natural that under closer examination complex phenomena can reveal even greater complexities that sometimes answer research questions bolder than those originally conceived. By answering the prescribed questions, the present study has cleared the way to understanding what conditions were responsible for leading to the results and what these results really tell us about hazardous waste crime. By probing further than the prescribed questions, we can convert this descriptive study into a much more utilitarian one.

At the heart of the present study are the questions: Who is the hazardous waste offender and how and why does he commit his offenses? Why do the answers to these questions vary for each sample state? (The sample states are all situated in the northeastern United States, yet the offenders within these states are unique in many ways, especially occupationally and in their methods of commission.)

The answers to the focal questions are determined by seven major factors:

- Industrial growth (extent and time period).
- Available disposal outlets (legal and illegal).
- Law enforcement response (extent and time period).
- The regulation/enforcement relationship.
- Visibility of offenses.
- The power of the criminal workplace.
- Syndicate crime/criminal complicity methods.

The rest of this chapter explains each of these factors and what impact they have on the characteristics of hazardous waste offenses and offenders.

Industrial Growth

One can properly separate the sample states into categories of low industrialization (Maine), medium industrialization (Maryland), and high industrialization (New Jersey and Pennsylvania). New Jersey is, and has been for a long time, industrially dominated by the chemical and petrochemical industries. Pennsylvania similarly boasts a long-standing petrochemical industry as well as extensive metal-product manufacturing. But it is easy to forget that certain regions of these two states, plus Maryland, are also home to a great many small generators. Survey research reminds us that 75 percent of the nation's small-quantity generators are located near major population centers, most being in the fields of vehicle maintenance and construction (Abt Associates Inc. 1985).

These factors spell out the disposal burden that has been carried by these states. Our sample of generating offenders indicates a high percentage of small generators (63 percent), but the minority of large generators have disposed more exorbitant volumes of wastes over longer periods. These sustained criminal actions have prompted a clarion call for toughened enforcement.

Of the sample, New Jersey experienced the largest and speediest growth of large generators. This escalated growth created both legal and illegal markets for disposal out of the necessity for perpetuating existing industries and continuing industrial growth. Maine, Maryland, and Pennsylvania witnessed a less organized effort to treat such wastes.

In the face of New Jersey's surging industrial growth, the hardening of regulatory laws and emergence of new criminal laws unintentionally contributed to the flourishing of its TSD facilities, both legitimate and illegitimate. To escape the heightened penalties for illegal disposal, New Jersey's generators were obliged to channel their wastes to TSD facilities. In effect, the core ingredient to the criminal act—the waste itself—had been transferred to a new type of caretaker. As these TSD offenders were identified by law enforcement authorities, the "official" offender in New Jersey began to take shape. Meanwhile, in states like Maine and Maryland, the urgency of industrial growth had not reached a point to warrant the development of a full-blown treatment industry. Unscrupulous generators in these states were found to resign themselves to using more convenient illegal outlets.

Available Disposal Outlets

Prior to New Jersey's first prosecuted cases, its hazardous waste offenders most likely were primarily generators. But the growing need for organized hazardous waste disposal in that state gave rise to an industry that could handle it—the treatment/storage/disposal industry. New Jersey's Hazardous Waste Siting Plan (Environmental Resources Management Inc. 1985) stresses that the TSD business is an interstate industry transporting and receiving wastes across state boundaries daily. Starting in the 1970s, New Jersey, its industry being much larger and more organized than other surrounding states, accepted substantial amounts of wastes from these states in addition to its own. Two of the highest-volume exporters to New Jersey facilities during the late 1970s and early 1980s were Pennsylvania and Maryland. The hazardous wastes most commonly exported to New Jersey from these states were nonhalogenated solvents (Environmental Resources Management Inc. 1985).

As the study has noted, during this time Pennsylvania lacked a single landfill approved for hazardous waste acceptance. Because of strict

Maryland regulations and the high number of medical research centers in the Baltimore and Washington, D. C., areas, these cities were forced to export medical wastes for proper treatment. But these were just parts of the total problem for Pennsylvania and Maryland. For these states, as well as for other states in the Mid-Atlantic and New England regions, New Jersey's TSD operators could name their price; as pointed out by interviewees, some saw the key to getting rich quick as the acceptance of mushrooming volumes of waste that required special treatment procedures. Many of these operators found they could unlawfully dispose fairly effortlessly because of enforcement vulnerabilities.

Maryland and Pennsylvania were becoming pressed between a growing industry base on one side and minimal legitimate state outlets on the other, and generators there had come to realize that New Jersey's TSD operators were controlling the region's waste disposal market. To many generators, especially small ones, exportation for waste treatment was financially prohibitive. Their solution frequently became the criminal improvisation of disposal outlets in their own states.

The vacuum of viable TSD industries in these states was eventually filled by informal business relations with landfill operators and with solid-waste haulers willing to take responsibility for disposal. In other cases the vacuum was filled by capitalizing on the state's topographical opportunities. In Pennsylvania, this meant dumping in secluded mining areas; in Maryland, in the farmlands; and in Maine, in the waterways. The uninspired or the cautious simply stockpiled until regulatory pressure required more overt criminal steps when the time was thought to be "right." Thus, the search for viable disposal outlets—more accurately, the failure of this search—had played its role in the shaping of the hazardous waste offender.

Law Enforcement Response

The time was right for illegal dumping when it became apparent that law enforcement activity and expertise had not caught up with that of the criminal. In New Jersey, the evidence shows that TSD operators were able to criminally dispose unhampered sometimes for more than a year before detection. This was largely possible because of the ineffectiveness and laxity of regulatory inspectors, who did little to match detection-avoidance inventiveness.

New Jersey and Pennsylvania's law enforcement responses to the offenses were a result of a social and legislative groundswell. And, although enforcers communicated with environmental agencies, the response came largely in the form of criminal enforcement to repel the offenses quickly and override the perceived faulty regulatory system. New Jersey began by targeting TSD facilities, for it saw them as criminally expanding in a world free of any true regulatory enforcement.

When enforcement task forces were activated in New Jersey and Pennsylvania, the two states were poised for a criminal justice response and followed through with it. In both states, lack of exposure to the hazardous waste field among those handling the cases sometimes resulted in flawed charging and prosecuting. Cases were lost because of unfamiliarity with local exemptions for disposal and difficulties in procuring proper evidence. Urged by public pressures to criminally charge whenever possible, a predisposition to the criminal enforcement side of the civil vs. criminal enforcement dichotomy exacted a cost in terms of relatively low prosecutorial success rates.

New Jersey's enforcement strategy must be viewed within the context of its being the earliest criminal enforcement tack assumed by any of the sample states. The steady evolution from early applications of "common nuisance" statutes to the adoption of a renovated criminal code reflects New Jersey's legislative and enforcement affinity for dealing with hazardous waste offenses on a criminal rather than a regulatory level. Anchored in this philosophy, New Jersey has invoked not only hazardous waste–specific criminal law but has been most aggressive in fusing them with more general white-collar crime statutes (for example, theft by deception, public-official misconduct) to intensify penalty potential.

New Jersey's enforcement history illustrates how discretionary enforcement can identify the criminal offender and where and how he operates. Originally faced with the realities of limited resources and personnel, New Jersey's hazardous waste enforcement unit marshaled its energies to attack those determined to be the most likely to dispose illegally in high volumes. New Jersey hoped to preempt those who were seen as conceivably inflicting the most harm to society by illegally disposing hazardous waste (TSD facility operators). This orientation toward the endpoint of the waste-treatment cycle is notably reflected in the occupational distribution of New Jersey's sample offenders.

Formed in the wake of New Jersey's and Pennsylvania's experiments, the task forces of Maine and Maryland were able to study the miscalculations and mishaps of the vanguard states. Their high prosecutorial success rates may, therefore, be a benefit of their later entrance into the hazardous waste enforcement field. It is plausible that it was also a fruit of their decision to merge environmental regulation and criminal enforcement rather than employ distinct and separate forms of enforcement.

The Regulation/Enforcement Relationship

By taking steps to unify environmental regulation and criminal enforcement, Maine and Maryland have, at a pole opposite to New Jersey and Pennsylvania, also helped fill in the picture of offense and offender in their states. Maine and Maryland's assistant attorneys general assigned to hazardous waste offenses all have emerged from environmental law backgrounds. In addition, Maryland formed an *autonomous unit* within the state's environmental' protection agency, and prosecuted both criminal and civil hazardous waste offense cases. Predictably, then, few communication or coordination troubles between criminal enforcement and regulatory enforcement actors were reported by criminal enforcement interviewees in Maryland. On another level, this avoidance of interagency strife helped raise success rates for both investigations and prosecutions of criminal cases and, finally, altered the picture of the state's known hazardous waste offenders as defined through official agency identification and legal processing.

It should be noted that the choice of enforcement unification in Maine and Maryland was made somewhat easier by conditions that did not exist in the other sample states. Industry was not burgeoning to the point where reactionary criminal enforcement positions were in order. Indeed, businesses in these states seemed to wield greater leverage to discourage criminal prosecution because of the relatively wider impact that corporate dissolution or relocation would have on local economies. Also, the states had experienced to a much lesser degree the hardships of a protracted period of regulatory ineffectiveness.

Along with the obvious pressures to prosecute criminally, the degree of historical success of regulatory agency actions help determine law enforcement's willingness to accept these actions as viable alternatives to criminal enforcement. In New Jersey and Pennsylvania, a chasm initially opened up between regulatory and criminal enforcement agencies as a result of law enforcement's perception of the failure of "cooperative regulation." As defined by Scholz's piece on the ecology of regulatory enforcement (1984), cooperative regulation stresses selective enforcement that takes into consideration the special circumstances of a violation. Under this philosophy it is assumed that each firm is innately "good." The corporation is allotted the "benefit of doubt" when a violation is suspected. In a cooperative regulation mode, regulatory inspections are infrequent, certain technical violations are overlooked, legitimate reasons for noncompliance are accepted, and generous abatement periods may be granted to correct serious violations. The system is based on trust and respect between firm and agency and on the assumption that the firm will act responsibly if it is given reasonable breaks or time to correct violations. Serious regulatory action does not occur until a series of prior warnings have been issued.

Bardach and Kagan (1982) point out that the most opportunistic firms will often capitalize on cooperative regulation to sidestep the costs of compliance. In New Jersey and Pennsylvania, criminal enforcers saw regulatory agencies' cooperative stratagems as opportunities for offending hazardous waste firms. A common complaint was that regulators were easily duped into believing firms were nonviolators. Criminal enforcers found it difficult to imagine how so many violations could go overlooked before a coercive response was taken.

The fact is that regulators had not accurately assessed conditions that Sholz maintains must be evaluated to effect successful cooperative enforcement. Regulators had not assessed the corporate "payoff" for noncompliance. Had they done so, they would have found that under a cooperative arrangement, financial benefits of illegal hazardous waste disposal far outweighed potential regulatory penalties. Regulators had simply not assessed the stability of environmental conditions. The upsurge in industrial output and TSD intake should have left little doubt that comers would be cut—illegally. Finally, regulators had not assessed their own ability to identify serious violations. They thus became players in a one-sided game where there was little incentive for firms to "cooperate."

The occasional cooptation of regulators by those regulated did not further the acceptance of regulatory agencies by criminal enforcement agencies. In the study, at least some environmental agents were found to be unable to escape the lure of such cooptation. Interviewees attested to the enticement of high salaries and prestigious employment positions offered to those operating in aspiration-stifling state bureaucracies. Stewart (1975) and Clinard and Yeager (1980) observe that attempts at complicity may be made more successful through an ease in pressure previously exerted by special interest constituencies. This diminishing of pressure is brought about by the misguided belief that the mere establishment of regulatory agencies presupposes effective regulation. These authors argue that the day-to-day influences and intimacies that develop between the regulator and regulated often mix with the regulator's sense of public apathy to create fertile ground for complicity.

In the end, what can be learned from the sample's enforcement experience is simple. One of the special, and for some enforcement personnel anguishing, aspects of hazardous waste enforcement is its dependence on interdisciplinary coalescence of regulatory and criminal enforcement and the exchange of knowledge between the two. Failure to thoroughly blend talents here can be a result of criminal enforcement agencies' resistance to regulatory cooperative tactics, inability to employ these tactics effectively, and cooptation by industry. What does this mean for hazardous waste crime? It means that in states where interagency cooperation is minimal, appropriate selectivity in criminal charging will suffer, resulting in higher volumes of criminal defendants but also higher rates of subsequent prosecutorial withdrawals, judicial dismissals, and/or acquittals. In these states, criminal enforcement, as a result of separatist stances, will sacrifice any hope that coalescence with even an imperfect regulatory agency could yield knowledge that would refine charging and redirect criminal enforcement resources away from inappropriate cases.

Visibility of Offenses

The fact that small generators far outnumber large generators in the U.S. is central to understanding the relatively high presence of small-generator offenders in the study's sample. However, interviewees argued that the prevalence of small generating firms within the total of waste-generating firms charged may also have been affected by factors such as relative ease of offense discovery and by the interrelated success of investigation and prosecution. Interviewees attributed the prevalence of small generators to the high visibility of criminal activity and clearer culpability of the offenders, as compared to large waste-generating firms, which are more apt to dispose on-site. Those interviewed sensed that large generating corporations would be less likely than small generators to form contractual agreements with outsiders (such as haulers, treaters) to dispose and treat wastes[1] and therefore devise formidable insulation from discovery by authorities. Enforcement inability to understand such industries' product-specific processes, of course, served to fortify the protective shield of on-site disposal.

These features of large industry generators and the obstacles they pose to effective investigation and prosecution of criminal behavior within them may supply insight into the apparent incongruity of results regarding sources of illegally disposed wastes. The sources of illegally disposed wastes in each state were some of the preeminent industries; paradoxically, while most of the wastes illegally disposed were generated by large chemical-producing and petrochemical companies, none of the criminally charged generators fell into these categories.

Although assessing hazardous waste crime solely from a perspective of the distribution of criminal incidents would "force" the designation of small generators as a high enforcement priority, such a focus would be misleading. To limit the most potential harm to life and environment, enforcement should look to the large generators as the true high-priority offenders.

The Power of the Criminal Workplace

The sample indicated the origin of "workplace crime" as fairly sporadic events growing over time into a more consuming pattern of behavior. Whereas criminal TSD executives underwent a transition with the motive of raising facility profits, the lower-level workers evolved from part-time to full-time crime as a requirement to maintaining employment. This criminality does not constitute independent "fiddling" as described by Mars (1982), for supplementing official salaries, but served as a means to ensure job security for the lower-level worker and unofficially to increase agency profits for the benefit of the executives and the business as a whole. In this respect, for criminal TSD facilities, the "grid" factor—management—and the "group" factor—coworkers—have the same criminal function and both merge to compel lower-level workers to join into the total reward system of TSD legitimate and illegitimate profits. Vaughan (1982) explains that this criminal socialization process of the firm employee is augmented when, as in the case of TSD facilities, the worker is unskilled and financially dependent.

Lack of sophisticated technical knowledge by business superiors and unorthodox criteria used for the hiring of subordinates are two factors that have been representative of corporations where unethical behavior runs rampant. Clinard (1983) and Evan (1976) claim that technically trained, "professional" workers are less likely to engage in unethical practices than those "financially oriented" types questing for instantaneous business success. Evan distinguishes between "fiduciary" executives who are loyal to high standards of ethics and to servicing beneficiaries, and "entrepreneurial" managers philosophically entrenched in total commitment to owners and to an optimal increase of profits.

Vaughan (1982) maintains that whatever the ruling philosophy of the firm, that orientation will be upheld through the methodical selection of new employees who would fit into these predetermined molds. This appears to be the case for TSD facilities and hauling firms, where lower-level employees are hired and segregated into criminal groups based upon their past criminal backgrounds. But a degree of naivete as to the danger of the offenses is also instrumental in the final identification of those most likely to be worthy candidates for offense execution.

From a utilitarian perspective, the most important question for the study of the hazardous waste crime workplace has to do not so much with whether the offender is professional or not, but what effect the criminal workplace has on TSD-facility operations and, in turn, what effect this has on public health. The study findings underscore the significance of a criminal subculture in the TSD workplace. Probably the most compelling discovery made here is that it is not unusual for criminality in the TSD workplace to pervade all employment ranks—in stark contrast to large generating companies, where criminality is typically confined to a fraction of executives and owners.

How can we apply this information to the enhancement of environmental protection? We are first obliged to take a closer look at individual TSD-facility criminal cases. In at least one case, TSD-facility criminal operations did not cease with the initiation of prosecuting procedures against some of its executives. We have also found that some operators run more than one offending TSD facility. With the public health in mind, we should be trying to guarantee that criminal activity is terminated with the prosecution of operators and prevented from continuing in other enterprises run by these operators (for example, the transferral of wastes from criminally prosecuted facilities to other owned facilities). The pervasiveness of crime in these facilities indicates that simply prosecuting one or two executives will not always crimp criminal offense activities.

The issue then is not one of putting individual criminal managers out of business but one of overthrowing the criminal subculture of the workplace itself. A suggested precaution for the prosecution of these facilities is to muster a joint effort of regulatory and law enforcement agencies to effect, through civil proceedings, state control over such operations concurrent with criminal proceedings.

As a preventive measure, we can expand the scope of laws that restrict licensing of those with criminal backgrounds who wish to become TSD operators (for example, New Jersey Statutes Annotated

13:1 E–126) to include that group most likely to have criminal backgrounds: TSD yard workers and drivers. As we have seen, these employees are often hired because of their criminal backgrounds to ensure future complicity. Perhaps with the interruption of the availability of such individuals, TSD-facility operators would find it more inconvenient to dispose illegally. TSD operators may be finally faced with the prospect of executing the offenses themselves. Judging from the study results, were they to become more aware of the potential for personal harm to crime executors, TSD operators might be less inclined to sacrifice their own safety for an increase in revenue.

Syndicate Crime/Criminal Complicity Methods

Up to the present, what little hazardous waste crime research there is has generally spotlighted the infiltrations of traditional, highly organized, syndicate crime families into the hazardous waste handling business, and has attempted to equate hazardous waste crime with syndicate crime. The presumption of absolute control of the industry by syndicate crime family figures has been accompanied by the reasoning that a crossover of solid waste industry offenders to the hazardous waste industry brought with it a system of "customer allocation." This study, however, found little evidence, based on criminal case analysis and enforcement personnel interviews, that syndicate crime had been successful in establishing a domineering control of the industry in the four-state sample.

The present study's design and results have helped to refocus the issue and, in doing so, to allow for a more exhaustive understanding of the offender's world and the significance of tightly woven, relatively small criminal networks in that environment. Rather than paint a limited portrait of the offender as professional racketeer, the data in this sample have provided an objective appreciation of the criminally heterogeneous world of the hazardous waste offender, one that entails peripheral actors (brokers, private laboratory technicians, regulatory inspectors, local public officials) who may intentionally or unknowingly contribute to the success of overt offenders.

A key value of the study then is its challenge to premature closure on the issue of syndicate crime domination; ultimately, this challenge can be instrumental in shaping enforcement tactics and perceptions of the industry as a whole. On this latter point, Reuter et al. (1983), in their study of racketeering in the solid waste and vending industries, have succinctly detailed the repercussions that may result from spurious conclusions on syndicate crime domination of an industry.

> The allegation once made tends to tarnish the reputation of almost all participants in the business. It thus acts as a barrier to entry into the industry of legitimate outsiders who wish to avoid acquiring an unsavory reputation. . . . Such allegations may act as a disincentive to financial institutions, fearful of doing business with crooks, from providing finance to the industry. . . . An industry's reputation as racketeer dominated may mean no more than the fact that years of law enforcement scrutiny have established contacts between people or corporations within the industry and recognized organized crime figures.

The visualization of hazardous waste crime within its business domain serves as a reference point for the examination of hazardous waste crime beyond the bounds of the syndicate crime issue. Following the lead of such authors as Sparks (1979) and Smith (1980), this open-ended route pursues a fuller understanding of the market structure and legitimate relationships within each particular business. The thrust of analysis becomes the misuse of legitimate forms of business to promote criminality rather than the orthodox "alien conspiracy" theory of organized crime.

It would be misguided, then, for law enforcement agencies to take as their task force goal for TSD facilities the complete mobilization against syndicate crime. However, the characteristic differences between "conventional" offending TSD facilities and facilities identified as being syndicate crime-connected warrants attention by the law enforcement community. Facilities identified as being syndicate crime-connected prove to be among the most flagrant offenders. In the sample, the four syndicate crime-connected facilities were found to have committed their offenses over four of the six longest periods of offense and represented four of the six highest TSD volume levels of unlawful disposal.

Syndicate crime-connected TSD facilities operate criminally for extended time periods—leading to exorbitant amounts of disposal—of their refined abilities to condition the legal environment to their liking. Some of the prominent features of such facilities are the very same features that permit successful evaluation of criminal detection and prosecution. Efforts orchestrated to compromise the positions of local and state regulatory officials were representative of syndicate crime-connected TSD facilities in the sample. By means of bribery and hiring of ex-regulatory officials, the operators of these facilities were able to erect formidable shields against criminal penalties. In effect, these operators were experts at carving out their own form of long-term immunity through the complicity of present regulatory officials and by tapping the legal experience of past officials.

One must be careful, though, not to conclude hastily that syndicate crime involvement was the chief factor determining grievous hazardous waste criminal behavior. One of the three TSD offending facilities with the longest periods of criminal offense and highest volumes of illegal disposal had no strong links to syndicate crime yet extensively used bribery, hiring of ex-city officials, bogus chemists, and brokers who would apply aggressive sales tactics in gaining the confidence of waste-generator customers. These features may stand as a trademark of TSD facilities connected to a syndicate, but, apparently, they can be just as easily employed by unconnected facilities if criminal initiative is strong enough. The key, then, to understanding the most serious hazardous waste offenses is not so much whether the facility can be unquestionably identified as infiltrated by syndicate crime but to what extent the operators depend on behavior patterns commonly associated with syndicate crime.

This information can be invaluable to the law enforcement community and particularly to the advancing of proactive enforcement. Investigators searching for markers that can help forecast the commission of blatant criminal violations might find it productive to focus on employment histories of major employees (in other words, past regulatory employment), associations with local public officials, as well as the professional and criminal backgrounds of the facility's "significant outsiders" (chemists, brokers, and so on). Naturally, further quantitative research—especially research employing comparisons to legitimate TSD businesses—would be necessary for a complete understanding of criminal connections and patterns.

Note

1. Two studies seem to support their contentions. Metz's 1985 report on hazardous waste enforcement and the Congressional Budget Office's 1985 document on hazardous waste management reveal 84 percent of generators ship their waste off-site, but this represents only 4 percent of the waste. Ninety-six percent is disposed on-site.

12

Prospects for the Future

Empirically designed research has afforded us a glimpse of who the hazardous waste criminal is, how he goes about committing his crimes, and how enforcement has fared in the struggle to limit his criminal activities. It would be naive, however, to believe that these characteristics would remain unchanged over time. Some important characteristics have already changed in the short time between the end of the initial four-state study and the follow-up close to three years later.

Follow-Up Survey Results

A follow-up survey of hazardous waste enforcement representatives from the original study's four sample states was conducted, also under the auspices of the Northeast Hazardous Waste Project. Besides input from these states, responses were solicited from enforcement representatives of ten other eastern states: Connecticut, Delaware, Massachusetts, New Hampshire, New York, Ohio, Rhode Island, Vermont, Virginia, West Virginia. Survey results indicated that there is now a better enforcement awareness of hazardous waste offender characteristics then there was at the time of the original study.

Overall, representatives of the original sample states reported that the characteristics of hazardous waste crime within the workplace had changed more in respect to the industries within which they occur than with respect to subcultural activities and systems. New Jersey's criminal enforcement crackdown on criminal TSD facilities, from the mid-1970s through the 1980s, effectively put much of this industry out of business. Nonetheless, hazardous waste criminality did not disappear in this state; it simply shifted to the generator phase or to other ancillary industries like the waste-oil and drum-reconditioning industries.

Hazardous waste offenders in the sample states were reported as being predominantly part of small- to medium-sized waste-generating companies relying more on internal clandestine criminal ventures than on disposal conspiracies with outside parties.[1] In some quarters, onsite releases were replaced with the stockpiling of wastes on generator land and the later abandonment on these properties. In New Jersey and Connecticut, these offenses were reported as being commonly committed by small waste-generating companies suffering through the final stages of bankruptcy.

"Significant outsiders" were still depended on to help neutralize detection and enforcement efforts; criminal socialization processes continue to be emblematic of the hazardous waste criminal milieu. As the siting and construction of new TSD facilities are slated for several of the sampled states, expectations are that a resurgence of the TSD industry minus accompanying intelligent enforcement could revive the industry's criminal subculture. Compared to its earlier years, the subculture now is relatively dormant.

Since the original study, hazardous waste crime had apparently changed in some areas, in terms of the methods of commission and the widening variety of substances constituting the wastes illegally disposed. Respondents from Delaware, Massachusetts, New Hampshire, Ohio, and Vermont indicated a marked rise in the criminal disposal of hazardous wastes in municipal sewer systems. In addition, Ohio, Pennsylvania, and Rhode Island noted that typical hazardous waste crime cases there are took on more of an interstate nature. With respect to the types of substances dumped, state respondents pointed to a rise in "gray area" offenses, such as medical wastes and shredder fluff from demolished motor vehicles. In these cases the hazardous quality of the substances is often questionable and must be decided on a case-by-case chemical content analysis.

From an enforcement perspective, probably the most encouraging result of the follow-up survey was the sign that progress was made toward the penetration of hazardous waste criminal systems. Enforcement interviewees acknowledged that employees of offending firms and neighbors of these companies were more forthcoming than ever in the local reporting of criminal disposal.[2] Some speculation was expressed that this could be a result of a combination of increased appreciation, by the general public and personnel of the firms, the physical threat of the offenses and the belief that criminal cases were more likely to reach successful disposition. This latter supposition is based on respondents' conclusions that the experience level of environmental officers has grown since the 1970s, making it less likely that cases will be lost because of investigative incompetence. Further, respondents believed that newly enacted state legislation has strengthened the environmental officer's hand in enforcing these cases.

In spite of the gains made in the investigation of hazardous waste offenses, hurdles to achieving consistency in prosecution success seemed to remain. The most frequently expressed prosecution-related problems dealt with difficulties in juror and judicial interpretation of complex criminal laws and regulations. In Ohio, Pennsylvania, Vermont, and Virginia this was particularly troublesome; juror and judicial uncertainty as to relevant laws and regulations was thought to jeopardize the attainment of guilty verdicts. Even in cases resulting in convictions, prosecutors in Virginia claimed that time spent on the courtroom clarification of the statutes resulted in substantial processing time delays.

Determinants of Future Crimes

Who, then, will be the hazardous waste offenders of the future? What will it take to bring their criminal actions under control? These are questions more and more on the minds of health officials, environmental regulators, and criminal prosecutors responsible for protecting the public from criminal dumpers. Based on what we now know about the hazardous waste offender, and the world within which he operates, some educated projections can be made on these subjects.

The characteristics of future hazardous waste offenders, and the crimes that they commit, will more than likely be determined by developments in several areas external to the criminal act: (1) pressure from the general public and public interest groups for stricter enforcement, (2) legislative expansion of the scope of legal coverage, (3) redesigned enforcement, and (4) future availability of affordable disposal outlets. These areas can be seen as the components of an equation that could lead to a reduction in hazardous waste crime. Regrettably, for now and for the foreseeable future, the equation is incomplete. We are, in fact, likely to see a heightening of offenses committed by medium and small generators throughout the Northeast and possibly the entire nation.

Since the original study was completed, we have seen changes in the types of environmental violations in the four states studied in the original *Dangerous Ground* project. Within the last few years, the state of Maine has experienced environmental problems in new areas. US taxpayers have paid more than $20 million to clean up after one Maine offender who engaged in the business of operating junkyards for military surplus materials. In this case, investigators discovered a discarded radioactive neutron generator, a tractor-trailer containing chemicals so reactive it spontaneously melted and various dangerous acids. Interestingly, the proliferation of the illegal methamphetamine trade has dramatically affected Maine. Maine's Clandestine Drug Laboratory Enforcement Team uncovered 4 meth labs in 2012. That increased to 16 labs in 2013 and 28 in 2014. The environmental threat there was manifested in the creation of methamphetamine "dump sites" throughout the state. At these sites, methamphetamine manufacturers illegally dispose of the toxic byproducts of the methamphetamine producing processes. The vast wooded areas of Maine provide perfect cover for these illegal operations. The same can be said for illegal dumping in Maine's state parks, which has recently risen. (Leary, 2015; Daley, 2005).

The same state park problem exists in present day New Jersey. There, illegal dumping has also been on the rise in the middle of the twenty-first century's second decade. A New Jersey Department of Environmental Protection (DEP) program to control illegal dumping in state parks and natural lands resulted in multiple arrests and charges throughout the state. Investigations of illegal dump sites in state parks were conducted by State Park Police, Conservation Officers, and the DEP's Compliance and Enforcement team. One earlier problem that returned to New Jersey after a several decade respite was the illegal dumping of medical waste. The most serious of these cases involved the disposal of needles and other medical-type waste that washed up on the beaches of Avalon, NJ resulting in the borough closing its beaches five times. The wastes included over 250 "Accuject" dental-type needles, 180 cotton swabs, a number of blue and white plastic capsules used to hold dental filling material, and other medical waste items. The offenders in this case were from Pennsylvania (Green, 2014; Thompson, 2010).

In the twenty-first century, Pennsylvania has seen a change in the types of environmental challenges faced. This new brand of environmental crime is closely associated with the increase of "fracking" operations in the state. Fracking involves shooting millions of gallons of water, sand and chemicals into shale rock. The objective is to break into deposits of precious natural gas. Unfortunately, a good portion of the waste liquid comes back to the surface. Naturally, like any other hazardous waste, this waste must be properly treated. Pennsylvania authorities are confronting cases where it has not been treated at all. The situation in modern day Maryland is a bit different. Many of the large environmental enforcement cases there have involved pollution from shipping or the large-scale filling of wetlands. One case entailed the criminal activities of civilian employees at the U.S. Army Aberdeen

Proving Ground, related to the dumping of hazardous chemicals. By and large, one of the greatest environmental concerns in Maryland today is agricultural waste runoff. (Begos, 2014; Kobell, 2012).

The Public's Growing Concern and Awareness

As time has passed, what many political strategists believed was the second wave of environmental politics should came to characterize the 1990s. Promotion of the passage of the Clean Air Act in March 1990, along with President George H. W. Bush's efforts to emphasize his image as an "environmental president," had helped sway many environmentalists into accepting the Bush administration as at least well-meaning. Voters in New Jersey elected the author of the nation's first superfund cleanup law, Jim Florio, their governor in November 1989—a victory that Florio's strategists claimed had more to do with his stand on the environment than any other issue. Results of a *New York Times*/CBS News poll conducted in April 1990 appeared to confirm this tenor of the public on a national level. In that poll, 74 percent of those polled said that protecting the environment was so important that requirements cannot be too high and that environmental improvements must be made at any cost. In a similar poll conducted in 1981 (Berke, 17 April 1990), only 45 percent held that belief.

Of course, survey results such as those were not lost on political candidates who struggled all the more to claim environmental protection issues as their own. Our political leaders, though, also realized, at the time, that the environmental interest groups and the public at large were expecting more from government than ever before—and this often translated into a call for stricter laws and enforcement.

Environmental groups in some northeastern states publicly urged citizens to support legislation that would impose mandatory jail sentences for repeat offenders (Gallagher, 18 May 1988). Groups like the National Environmental Law Center (NELC) formed to furnish environmental groups with the legal and scientific expertise to fight polluters in court. Those in charge of these legal assistance organizations believed that environmental enforcement should expand nationally and multinationally to meet the expansion of corporations (Burroughs, 25 July 1990). This groundswell made it easy to understand why the 15th Annual Economics Summit of the seven leading industrialized nations became known as the "Green Summit"— focusing for the first time in the history of these summits on global environmental issues (Rast, 10 July 1989).

Change in the Scope of Legal Coverage

Hazardous waste crime in the four sample states will assume even greater proportions in the future than it has in the past. The basis for this prediction is grounded in the current and projected changes in criminal law. In short, the scope of hazardous waste handling activities that fall into the category of regulatory and criminal violations will widen as hazardous waste capacity shortfall worsens.

Certain amendments to the Resource Conservation and Recovery Act (RCRA) are chief factors in the marked increase in the scope of federal regulation of the hazardous waste field (Pub. L. No. 98–6161, 1984 U.S. Code Cong. & Ad. News, 98 stat., 3221, amending the Resource Conservation and Recovery Act of 1976, 42 U.S. C., 6901–6987, 1982). For example, previously unregulated underground storage tanks will now be regulated for leakage. It is estimated that, nationally, 75,000 to 100,000 such tanks are now leaking and 350,000 may develop leaks by the mid-1990s (Mugdan and Adler 1985; 130 Cong. Rec. Hill, 140, 1984). The amendments also impose stricter standards on the production, sale, and use of waste oil and mandate corrective actions on inactive units of operating facilities. In the past, the regulation of such inactive units fell through the cracks. CERCLA (Comprehensive Environmental Response, Compensation, and Liability Act of 1980, 42 U.S. C., 9601–9657, 1982) was previously employed to address abandoned disposal sites while RCRA concentrated on the regulation of new and existing facilities. Neither confronted the problem of closed units of active facilities. Apparently, lost time is meant to be made up here.

In New Jersey, the implementation of revised standards for underground storage tanks put industry officials under the gun to upgrade the tanks by tight deadlines. A New Jersey Department of Environmental Protection Agency estimate maintained that only one third of New Jersey's underground tanks holding petroleum and hazardous materials complied with the standards. Upgrading of the tanks had been estimated at $50,000 to $100,000 for the average service station owner.

The RCRA amendments also "created" new crime areas. Most notably, these involve the knowing violations of interim status standards for existing TSD facilities, the exportation of hazardous wastes to another country without consent of that country, or the violating of international procedures on such exportation (Pub. L. No. 98–616, section 232, 1984 U.S. Code Cong. & Ad. News, 98 Stat., 3256–57).

Probably most significant of all these amendments is section 221, the amendment dealing with small-quantity generators. The amendment in effect lowers the cut-off volume level of those previously exempt from EPA regulations because of low levels of waste generation. This is exactly the sort of action demanded by some scholars to bring the law into step with hazardous waste management problems that, if ignored, could damage the credibility of hazardous waste management in general.

Congress took what amounted to unusually stern steps in enacting the RCRA amendments because of the EPA's past failures in meeting its regulatory mandates. However, tightening the regulatory net can easily have the reverse effect of provoking the selection of criminal dumping to avoid detection of regulatory violation. To comply with revised standards, those possessing leaking underground storage tanks and/or inactive units of operating facilities, those handling waste oil, and those exporting hazardous waste to other countries must now incur additional expenses to comply with new regulations. To many hazardous waste generators and handlers, this will be financially prohibitive and will elevate the desirability of illegal dumping as an alternative to regulatory compliance. The amendments should have their most important impact, in this respect, on those previously exempt small-quantity generators who must now devote resources to treat wastes that may have been stored on business premises for years. The presence of the new amendments provides a strong incentive to dispose criminally for these small-quantity generators whose businesses may crumble financially under the weight of newly imposed regulatory standards.

Hazardous waste offenders charged since the original study and the follow-up survey continue to fit the description of small-business waste generators grappling with "cost-effective" alternatives to legitimate treatment or independent, enterprising individuals seeking to cash in on the dearth of legitimate disposal outlets. More than ever, tightening of environmental laws and regulations is having the unintended effect of forcing those unaccustomed to considering the commission of criminal actions to do just that. In some cases the impacts are and will be industry-wide. The services rendered by these industries are often those that have come to be expected by a public that also demands protection from waste contamination.

A good example of these industries is the electroplating business. Electroplaters treat practically all metal materials used in our present mechanized society to ward off rust and corrosion. The problem is that the treatment process, which involves bathing the metal in sulfuric acid and plating agents, leaves a hazardous residue. Since an EPA ban on the landfilling of these wastes, electroplaters throughout the nation have been expected to find other means for disposal that are often financially disastrous. Many find they cannot pay the high costs of treatment and remain competitive at the same time. Environmentalists, largely responsible for applying pressure for the introduction of the landfilling ban, concede that not enough has been done by government or industry researchers to provide affordable treatment technology to electroplaters. Consequently, electroplaters wishing to obey the law have been confronted with a perplexing situation.

As described previously with regard to shredder wastes, new gray areas of hazardous waste disposal have become more clearly defined as criminal as we go through the twenty-first century. One such area is medical waste, which, when discovered to be illegally disposed, can elicit a fear of causing such harm as to prompt immediate and severe legal action. Events like the huge 1987 garbage slick that shut down New York and New Jersey beaches became catalysts for state attorneys general to combat medical-waste dumping. The initial Ocean Pollution Conference set an agenda for the strict enforcement of existing water standards and environmental laws that had a history of being consistently ignored by many municipalities and sewerage authorities. Although representatives at the conference were quick to emphasize the importance of illegal midnight dumping and downplay the concentrated media blitz on medical-waste dumping, it was this latter category that received more legislative attention and resulted in tight restrictions on its disposal.

The repeated incidents of medical waste—blood vials, syringes, and other debris—washing up on beaches prompted the signing of a bill creating a pilot program to track medical-waste disposal in Connecticut, New Jersey, New York, and the Great Lakes states. The law required fines up to $50,000 a day and incarceration of up to five years for violators of the program. It also gave the EPA access to the records of all facilities generating medical waste in the areas covered by the program.

Redesign of Enforcement

Since the initial study, over 20 states created environmental enforcement task forces, modeled after Maryland, New Jersey, and Pennsylvania programs. The New Jersey task force matured to a point where they developed the expertise to successfully pursue large corporations capable of hiding their environmental crimes. Federal authorities also become more willing participants in the criminal enforcement of hazardous waste offenses. At the time of the publication of this edition (2015), however, it has become clear that a number of these states have "rolled back" their support of such task forces in times of resource shortages and shuffling of state priorities.

As was seen with the four sample states of the study, hazardous waste enforcement task forces evolved as the offspring of two dichotomies: (1) civil vs. criminal enforcement and (2) merged environmental regulation and criminal enforcement vs. distinct and separate forms of enforcement. The most effective of the four state programs was Maryland's, which demonstrated a balancing of civil and criminal enforcement approaches and an overlapping of regulatory and criminal enforcement responsibilities where deputy attorneys general prosecute cases both civilly and criminally. Because this merging of responsibilitiess worked so admirably in Maryland, other states strove to replicate these structures to decrease enforcement duplication and increase enforcement productivity.

However, In December of 2012, Rena Steinzor and Aimee Simpson from Maryland's Center for Progressive Reform, co-authored a report entitled *Going Too Easy? Maryland's Criminal Enforcement of Water Pollution Laws Protecting the Chesapeake Bay*. In it they stated that state and federal prosecutors in Maryland had backpedalled from their positions as national leaders resulting in fewer cases and softer penalties. The reasons given were budget cuts and shifting priorities. In the 1990s, the U.S. Attorney's office in Maryland fielded a vibrant environmental prosecution team. But, by the end of 2001 the environmental crimes team was disbanded. Former President George W. Bush insisted that U.S. attorneys focused almost exclusively on terrorism and homeland security. Several of the attorneys moved into private practice. Today, many of the state level prosecutions focus on point-source pollution (e.g. oil or sewage discharges from pipes into a bodies of water). Across the Bay watershed, agriculture is said to account for over 30 percent of the nitrogen, 40 percent of the phosphorous, and 50 percent of the sediment, making it the largest pollution sector for Maryland. The Center's report strongly recommends enhanced enforcement, improved coordination between the agencies and increased funding for staff to investigate environmental crimes in Maryland (Kobell, December 1, 2012).

Some states have divided responsibilities once under one roof to create more specialized units for hazardous waste enforcement and regulation. But the federal government, and some states, have seen fit to merge certain regulatory and criminal enforcement responsibilities under the direction of specially appointed environmental prosecutors.

The decision to merge forces under a single environmental prosecutor has certainly had its critics. After the failure to indict three managers of the Ciba-Geigy pharmaceutical company for illegal hazardous waste disposal, state assembly Democrats prodded New Jersey's governor, to create a special prosecutor position to prosecute such cases. They argued that the cases should be removed from the attorney general's control and placed in an office owing no allegiance to any one elected official to avoid being mismanaged for the advancement of political goals. The position remained within the attorney general's office and, more significantly, attorneys from the state Department of Environmental Protection were transferred to the attorney general's office over objections voiced by DEP attorneys and 14 state environmental organizations. The official reason for these moves was expressed as improving the coordination of enforcement efforts and affording the state a centralized legal service against environmental violations. But, New Jersey eventually retrenched, and the special prosecutor position was ultimately eliminated.

Availability of Treatment/Disposal Options

The final element of the hazardous waste crime equation is the level of governmental competency in effectively supplying viable treatment/disposal options for hazardous waste generators. In an attempt to make up for the lack of available treatment facilities, northeastern states like New Jersey began looking toward exporting hazardous wastes across their borders into other states. A survey conducted by INFORM, a Manhattan-based nonprofit research organization, revealed that New Jersey, Pennsylvania and Ohio were the top three net exporters of hazardous waste. All of the top five net importing states—Louisiana, Alabama, Tennessee, Michigan, and Indiana—were southern or midwestern states. Not one northeastern state was a net importer. Since the mid-1980s, hazardous waste volume in most states has increased while availability of legitimate outlets for their disposal has either stayed the same or decreased. The New Jersey Hazardous Waste Facilities Plan forecasted that New Jersey's demand for treatment/disposal would be more intense because of (1) wastes generated from inactive disposal site cleanups, (2) the closing of some on-site facilities, (3) stricter regulations on land emplacement facilities, and (4) stricter regulations on industrial waste water and pretreatment.

At the very least, it is obvious that foreseeable legal developments and disposal outlet conditions warrant little optimism that hazardous waste crime will decrease. Without the creation of new treatment and disposal outlets at the local level, these states are in danger of unwittingly helping to produce a whole new population of hazardous waste criminals. More hazardous waste will be generated, while fewer storage and disposal methods used in the past will be considered acceptable and seemingly few new TSD facilities will emerge to meet the increased demands. In essence, the future hazardous waste criminal, at least in the Northeast, should prove to be one whose criminal profit motive will often be equaled by the motive simply to elude penalties for regulatory violation in an area of limited legitimate alternatives to criminal disposal.

This not only portends a higher frequency of generator offenses but, out of the necessity of detection avoidance, a reliance on more intricately improvised methods of criminal commission of those previously used by TSD offenders (for example, "savior" installations). It is anticipated that some large-quantity generators, realizing their potential for increased treatment/disposal capacities and their ability to isolate themselves from effective enforcement, will themselves become semicommercial facilities. They would criminally profit from the scarceness of new TSD facilities by accepting other generators' waste and then disposing illegally. Though this is somewhat speculative, it is expected that hazardous waste crime concentration could, for a state like New Jersey, travel full circle from the TSD operator/employee back to the hands of the generator, given the changes in legal and economic circumstances.

Horizons for Hazardous Waste Crime Enforcers

Given the ever-increasing volumes of generated hazardous wastes and the growing popularity of public interest groups dedicated to eliminating environmental pollution, it has become de rigueur to predict that we cannot win the battle against illegal dumping unless more laws are passed and criminal enforcement is made more aggressive. Such views reflect a widespread sense that we will be overtaken by the organized criminality of polluters if we do not keep the heat of the legal system on them. And yet a trend is emerging that may give the doomsayers pause. If we are to believe the average small-business waste generator, the zeal with which we seek to widen and strengthen the criminal enforcement net may prove to be the single most significant factor in fostering exactly that behavior we wish to prevent.

119

It is clear that, until enforcement agency representatives assume a more wide-ranging role in public awareness of treatment needs, the promotion of realistic siting options, and source reduction, purveyors of justice may become their own worst enemy. The hazardous waste crime fighter can no longer afford to ignore generator dilemmas borne of a system in which burgeoning waste amounts meet a dead end of few viable treatment/disposal outlets. The effective hazardous waste crime enforcer of the future will be obliged to wear several hats, permitting him to cross disciplinary boundaries to accomplish the more comprehensive, long-range goals of environmental protection.

A commitment on the part of law enforcement to forestall the growth of hazardous waste crime must progress responsively; it must display an ongoing awareness of (1) the hazardous waste disposal/treatment industry; (2) economic trends affecting this industry; (3) early targeting of financially faltering facilities/firms; (4) the identification of potential crime areas heretofore untouched by enforcement; (5) local treatment facility siting developments; (6) longitudinal studies of trends in methods of commission; and (7) longitudinal studies of variations in methods of offense discovery (abrupt changes in this last area can trigger shifts in offense commission methods).

These efforts notwithstanding, the absence of complementary legislative action toward the closing of defined enforcement gaps can debilitate systematic advancements. Possibilities of government regulation or assumption of services provided by secondary network actors, such as treatment brokers, requires exploration, as does the targeting of ex-hazardous waste offenders entering such industry-related, nonregulated fields. In addition, the critically exploitable deficiencies inherent in the present manifest tracking system must be seriously addressed.

A common, almost obligatory, suggestion arising where the targeted crime area is seen as unmanageable, or on the brink of being so, is a summoning of resource enhancements. While the sheer escalation of personnel volume is clearly an aid, by itself it constitutes a half-hearted gesture in light of the abstractions of hazardous waste crime. A practical enforcement approach to the contextual environment of hazardous waste crime remains incomplete without creativity in personnel development. This creativity calls for a realigning of the strictly defined parameters of the law enforcer role to reach beyond simple investigative-techniques training. For proactive enforcement, hazardous waste law enforcers will need to fortify assistance obtained from environmental agency interactions and establish a mastery of subjects such as treatment market structures, industrial production processes, and changes in regulations influencing them, as well as a wider base of knowledge in waste chemical properties. To prepare for any regional displacements of hazardous waste crime, law enforcers must be proficient in these topics not only for their home states but also for bordering states.

The present study was intended to help criminal justice decision makers stand outside the crime area and question routine ways of targeting, investigating, and prosecuting hazardous waste crimes. This chapter has offered some ideas for enriching enforcement production; naturally, it is not all-inclusive. It is sincerely hoped that study results will kindle meaningful enforcement introspection, help point to new strategies, and enable state programs to realize their full potential.

Even if state and federal enforcement agencies are successful in merging criminal-law and environment-protection interests, it would be a serious oversight not to include local enforcement agencies as part of this coordinating effort. Logically, the focus of environmental regulations has shifted from the overriding past concern with large facility discharges to the discharges of a much greater number of small facilities. Evolving laws and regulations covering a vast regulated universe pose obvious enforcement problems for future enforcers on all government levels—federal, state, and local.

Based on "sources of discovery" results from the this study and their own study of local government, the EPA fashioned an initiative that encouraged an expanded local government role in a six-point plan that would:

(1) Identify regulatory areas amenable to local government participation.
(2) Determine functions local government could perform to facilitate effective environmental enforcement.
(3) Identify which local governments might play a larger role.
(4) Develop local institutions to guide local governments.
(5) Develop training to help identify environmental crimes.
(6) Foster greater local district attorney involvement in criminal prosecutions.

Directly after the release of this study's findings, the leaders of the EPA came to realize how indispensable are the enforcement resources provided by local government. Out of necessity, the EPA progressed beyond the confining view of local government's value as solely the eyes and ears of federal government enforcement and has began to recognize the importance and potential of local criminal enforcement in its own right. The EPA openly encouraged the rigorous local prosecution of environmental offenses as a means of contending with the anticipated surge in small-facility violations. As the EPA saw it, the number of these violations became too large for serious attention by the EPA or even state enforcement agencies.

This is why the EPA placed so much of its faith in the prosecutorial abilities and information exchange of local district attorneys and their investigative staffs. The drafters of EPA's altered approach clearly understand that local prosecutors will need federal support if they are truly to make some impact on the environmental crime problem. This means enhanced training and improved laboratory and technical resources—all promised through the EPA's initiative. It also meant adopting a more proactive posture in the EPA's relations with local prosecutors.

To carry forward this proactive strategy, it was recommended that EPA, in cooperation with the U.S. Department of Justice, develop a network with the National District Attorneys Association (NDAA), the National Association of Attorneys General (NAAG), and other local prosecution and regulation organizations to explore:

(1) Establishing criteria for screening environmental offense cases.
(2) Conducting exemplary practices projects.
(3) Developing a centrally located computerized system to collect local crime statistics on a nationwide basis.
(4) Analyzing collected data to develop an environmental crime profile.

In the wake of this recommendation, NDAA created an Environmental Protection Committee of local prosecutors to help address the above issues. Efforts such as theserepresent but a few steps along the road to improved environmental enforcement, the nexus of which is optimal coordination and communication among federal, state, and local enforcement agencies. Given the magnitude of the environmental issues facing the nation, it is apparent that these efforts were sorely needed.

Notes

1. Pennsylvania respondents postulated that the increase in these on-site related offenses could be attributed to an avoidance of the growing costs of transportation inherent in generator/disposer conspiratorial arrangements for illegal dumping.

2. This phenomenon was experienced by respondents from Connecticut, Maryland, Massachusetts, New York, Pennsylvania, Virginia, and West Virginia. Local reporting sources also included municipal police, competitors of offending firms, and anonymous informants.

Epilogue

The Growing Menace and the Fight to Contain It

In the epilogue to the original edition of *Dangerous Ground*, illegal hazardous waste disposal was described as a variation of one long game of "hot potato." That feature of illegal hazardous waste disposal remains the same to this day. In this toxic gambit, the criminal goal is to make as much profit as one can by being the *temporary* possessor of the "hot potato" before unloading it on some other person, organization, or place. In the end, the final recipient is the loser. It may turn out to be the new owner of a single-family dwelling, a business that has moved to a new location contaminated by the previous owner, or, ironically, the enforcement agency investigating environmental crimes. Ultimately, some entity pays the final price of being the eventual direct "victim" of wastes that are usually generated through a legal manufacturing process; a process that often produces consumer-related products that are in high demand. Frequently, the destinations of these wastes become those states that are willing to accept burgeoning waste volumes from other states not fully equipped to handle them. During the period of the original publication of this book, the exportation of New Jersey hazardous wastes destined for out-of-state treatment met with a public backlash in several Midwestern states, and some popular "waste destination" states were battling in the courts to erect barriers against the flagrant importation of hazardous wastes.

The typical products in demand may have changed since the 1990s when *Dangerous Ground* was first published, but the fundamental chain of events that lead to typical illegal dumping are largely unchanged. While much of the book's contents on hazardous waste crime are confined to illegal activities in the northeastern United States, the reader should not conclude that the problem was less serious in other parts of the country at the time or, for that matter, in other parts of the world. Indeed, recent evidence indicates that massive hazardous waste

123

generation and the inevitable pollution that accompanies it have left few geographic areas untouched. Both the illegitimate and legitimate games of hazardous waste "hot potato" are taking place every day—between individuals, businesses, cities, counties, states, and now, even countries. At present, we know that the "hot potato" syndrome has expanded geographically to become an international one, with, in many cases, wastes being sent abroad from the U.S. to other less-developed countries as the final repository.

Lately, INTERPOL has been especially attentive to the growing export of wastes derived from electronic equipment such as computers, cell phones and other electronic mobile devices. The proliferation of exporting of this "e-waste" or WEEE (waste electrical and electronic equipment) is propelled by differential costs associated with the treatment and regulation of e-waste in destination nations and lax enforcement in those importing countries. There currently is a great demand for e-waste in these countries, particularly on the African continent, because the costs of purchasing new electronic equipment is often prohibitive, creating a large market for used electronic materials. In many cases, repair of this used equipment is found to be impossible, and those used parts are then indiscriminately dumped in landfills not properly equipped for receiving such waste, endangering the health of the general population (INTERPOL, 2013). The U.S. Attorneys Office of the District of Colorado has demonstrated that it can be tough on offenders. In 2013, Executive Recycling, Inc. and its owner and chief executive officer were sentenced for fraudulent schemes related to the disposal and exportation of electronic waste to foreign countries. Executive Recycling was an electronic waste recycling business that collected electronic waste from private households, businesses, and government entities and exported electronic waste from the United States to countries like the People's Republic of China. The company was sentenced to pay a $4.5 million fine and its owner was sentenced to 2.5 years in a federal prison, followed by 3 years on supervised release.

In 2014 the environmental crime spotlight was focused on the mistreatment of wastes from hydraulic fracturing ("fracking"), in which rock is fractured by a hydraulically pressurized liquid to get at precious natural gas or petroleum. In September of 2014, an Exxon Mobil Corp subsidiary was charged by the Pennsylvania state attorney general for spilling more than 50,000 gallons of fracking wastewater. The subsidiary was charged with spilling chemical-laced wastewater from a storage tank and into a local waterway. Pollutants from the chemically treated water—including chlorides, barium, and strontium—were dumped into a tributary of the Susquehanna River, the same destination of some of the more insidious offenses from the Pennsylvania cases studied in the original study *Dangerous Ground* was based on, over 20 years ago (Reuters, 2014). Also in 2014, the owner of a Pennsylvania company responsible for moving waste and equipment for the natural gas industry, along with many of his family members, were charged with environmental crimes and insurance fraud by the Pennsylvania's Attorney General's Office. The charges involved the alleged dumping and burying of fracking wastes and overbilling of contractors in several Pennsylvania counties.

This updated edition of *Dangerous Ground* is being published on the heels of renewed attention to the part major corporations can play in notorious environmental offenses. In January 2013, BP Exploration and Production Inc. (BP) was sentenced to pay $4 billion in criminal fines and penalties after pleading guilty to 11 counts of felony manslaughter, one count of felony obstruction of Congress, and violations of the Clean Water and Migratory Bird Treaty Acts for its role in the 2010 Deepwater Horizon oil rig disaster that killed 11 people and the subsequent oil spill that resulted in the largest environmental disaster in U.S. history. In the four years since the blowout, BP had spent more than $28 billion on damage claims and cleanup costs. Despite the admissions of guilt, BP had insisted that it was not chiefly responsible for the accident, and that its contractors were largely to blame. On September 4, 2014, a federal judge in New Orleans rejected the BP claims, and determined that BP was the primary responsible party and that the company had rejected known risks and that its actions were grossly negligent opening the possibility of $18 billion in civil penalties for BP, nearly quadruple the maximum Clean Water Act penalty for simple negligence. The judge chided BP for is frantic attempts to shut down an over budget drilling operation that was behind schedule calling it a "chain of failures" leading to the deadly explosion and massive oil spill (Robertson and Krauss, September 5, 2014). Environmental crime was, once again, in the news. Unfortunately, such aggressive government actions are not necessarily the norm.

Recently the world's largest company by revenue pled guilty to serious environmental violations. Walmart, headquartered in Bentonville, Arkansas, has over 11,000 stores in 27 countries, under a total 71 different brands. It is the biggest private employer in the world with over two million employees, and the largest retailer in the world. Yet, it is not immune from participating in environmental desecrations. In May of 2013, Walmart Stores Inc. pled guilty to cases filed by federal prosecutors in Los Angeles and San Francisco involving the illegal handling and disposing of hazardous materials at its retail stores across the United States. Walmart paid over $81 million for its violations. Combined with payments for similar violations in California, Walmart paid a combined total of more than $110 million for their environmental offenses. The U.S. Justice Department's Environment and Natural Resources Division charged that Walmart put the public and the environment at serious risk besides gaining an unfair economic advantage over competitive companies. Nationwide, Walmart sells thousands of products that fit the definition of being flammable, corrosive, reactive, toxic, or otherwise hazardous under federal law. These products contain hazardous materials that include pesticides, solvents, detergents, paints, aerosols, and cleaners. The products are considered hazardous waste under federal law once they are discarded. According to the U.S. Attorney's Office for the Western District of Missouri, truckloads of hazardous products, including more than two million pounds of pesticides, were improperly handled by Walmart. The criminal cases were the result of collaborative investigations conducted by the FBI and the EPA with assistance from the California Department of Substance and Toxics Control, and the Missouri Department of Natural Resources (U.S. Department of Justice, 2013).

Another recent example of purported environmental recklessness by corporate America, involves Duke Energy. Duke Energy, headquartered in Charlotte, North Carolina, is the largest electric power holding company in the United States, with assets also in Canada and Latin America. In February of 2015, federal prosecutors filed criminal charges against Duke Energy accusing the company of violating the federal Clean Water Act by illegally dumping millions of gallons of toxic coal ash into the Dan River in North Carolina. Coal ash is a waste product from generating electricity. The resulting waste contains heavy metals including lead, arsenic, selenium and mercury. In this incident, millions of gallons of toxic coal ash slurry poured through a rupture in a 48-inch concrete storm pipe that ran underground. During a six-day period before the leak was plugged, more than 35 million gallons of slurry had leaked, coating the riverbank as far as 70 miles down the river toward Danville, Va. In a situation that some would term "environmental racism," many of the plants found to be improperly handling the waste were near poor and black communities. The primary regulating agency, the North Carolina Department of Environment and Natural Resources, was accused by activists of "protecting" Duke Energy. The agency had recently gone through a series of budget cuts and layoffs prior to the spill. Charges of state political "cronyism" were also leveled by environmental activist groups (Katz, 2015).

Throughout most of the 1970s and 1980s, it was fashionable in the U.S. to criticize the use of criminal sanctions against hazardous waste offenders as unwarranted. Civil enforcement was favored at the local and federal levels of the United States, as well as in other nations. In the mid to late 1990s and the early years of the twenty-first century, our government leaders seemed to be seeing the light, and criminal enforcement of hazardous waste offenses was finally coming of age, and with good reason. Crime control study groups, like the Law Reform Commission of Canada, were integral to identifying the societal benefits of criminal prosecution for these offenses. These included the intrinsic benefits of *specific* deterrence of those being criminally prosecuted and the *general* deterrence of those who would contemplate the commission of these acts. At the time, it was widely believed that criminal prosecution would send a forceful message to the community that these activities would not be tolerated and build public trust that prosecutors would effectively be representing the will of the public. It was also thought that criminal prosecution could become a source of encouragement for the reporting of the offenses. The conventional wisdom was that increased frequency of criminal prosecutions would foster a higher level of public assimilation of the concept of hazardous waste dumping as "crime" and increase the likelihood that citizens would accept responsibility for reporting such incidents.

At the time of the original publication of *Dangerous Ground*, the EPA and the U.S. Department of Justice were forging ahead to put more bite into criminal enforcement/prosecutions. William Reilly, administrator of the EPA at the time, promised to initiate a higher frequency of criminal prosecutions resulting in more serious fines and prison sentences. As he announced, "If you break the law, you're going to pay. Environmental crimes are every bit as serious as any other kinds of crime" (*USA Today*, 3 April 1991). Hiring practices at the EPA in the early 1990s seemed to indicate Reilly intended to be true to his word. In 1992, the EPA had 60 criminal investigators, compared to 23 in 1982, and planned to raise that figure to 500 in the future. The U.S. Department of Justice similarly beefed up its number of prosecutors.

Sadly, it appears that we may, in some ways, be retreating from this position in the mid-2000s. Noted criminologists have argued that the EPA has an unmanageable mandate with inconsistent support. As an explanation, they point to the combined impact of efforts to respond to various power groups, a widening range of environmental threats and fierce competition to maintain satisfactory levels of resource funding (Burns, Lynch and Stretesky, 2008). It appears that former EPA administrator William Reilly's 1991 prediction of raising the number of EPA investigators to 500 may never be realized. In July of 2014, journalist Graham Kates, reported that the agency had less than half that number. Kates also lamented the fact that the Department of Justice's Environmental Crimes Section had only 38 prosecutors for the entire country. (Kates, 2014). Individuals like Graham Kates have been instrumental in scrutinizing the activities of the EPA and criticizing the agency for not doing enough to control and deter environmental crime in the U.S. His review of public records in 2013 revealed that more than 64,000 facilities listed by the Environmental Protection Agency (EPA) were in violation of federal environmental laws, yet only 297 were found to have been investigated for crimes. He observes that the numbers of federal criminal investigations have steadily declined since 2001. Graham's research was able to elicit comments from an EPA spokesperson that the declining trend is a result of a deliberate decision by the agency to dedicate its resources to high profile cases in light of staff reductions and budget cuts. (Kates, 2014)

There is some evidence that such has been the case at the state and local levels too. In *The State of Environmental Crime Prosecution* in New York, James J. Perricone asserted that there is evidence that local prosecutions of environmental crimes has fallen in the twenty-first century. He attributes this, largely, to two factors: the reluctance of judges and juries to support sentences of incarceration for these crimes and a growing level of complicity between state governments and the business world. He traces the reluctance to impose jail time as an outgrowth of the general public's greater concern with traditional person-to-person street crime than crimes against the environment. The theory he has presented is that, in light of the media's heavy coverage of violent and terroristic acts, the public has become somewhat jaded when it comes to crimes against the environment. He posits that criminal enforcement is consistently being replaced with civil enforcement resulting in higher fines and an embracing of a "compliance model" of environmental violation control (Periconi, 2009).

However, presently, there are still examples of local prosecutor offices that continue to maintain an aggressive stand against environmental crimes. The most noteworthy one is in California. The Los Angeles County District Attorney's Office prides itself on reporting that one of its top priorities is to increase the office's focus on investigating and prosecuting environmental crimes. The Los Angeles County District Attorney's Environmental Law Section works with local, state and federal agencies to address environmental issues and investigate criminal matters. The office prosecutes those who harm the county's environment and its residents by violating rules and laws designed to protect them, as well as those businesses that gain unfair advantage over their competitors by circumventing the rules. As reported by the LA County DA's Office, some of the more common environmental offenses investigated and prosecuted include the following: the illegal transportation, treatment, storage or disposal of hazardous waste; oil spills and other discharges of toxic substances; fraudulent certification of automobile smog tests; the emission of hazardous and dangerous chemicals into the air, water and soil; death and serious injuries to employees whose employers fail to comply with safety regulations. This office has undertaken a highly effective training program for environmental crimes investigators. The training program teaches investigators how to effectively prepare reports for cases to be submitted for prosecution. According to officials at this office, these trainings have helped yield better quality cases, aiding the prosecution of those who violate environmental laws and holding these offenders accountable for their actions. The Office also prosecutes workplace safety crime and has obtained numerous criminal convictions for Occupational Safety and Health Act (OSHA) violations.

Besides addressing the problem of declining investigations and prosecutions of environmental crimes, more attention must be paid to realistic methods of imposing sanctions. Historically, judges have been reticent to hand down sharp penalties for hazardous waste crimes. Often the crimes are seen as undeserving of strict sanctions because they are characterized as economic crimes that may be committed unknowingly. This position must change drastically before we see substantial change in the criminal activity patterns of the offenders. Levels of risk and harm must be reasonably equated with levels of punitive sanctions and be administered accordingly. Also, we should not fall into the trap of singling out risk and direct harm as the only standards by which the severity of sanctions should be judged. Considerations

129

like the gradual deterioration of the ecosystem and infringement on what can be agreed upon as a normal state of living conditions must be taken into account. It is time that stringent sanctions, including punitive fines and imprisonment, using such standards are more consistently imposed so that we may experience a demonstrable deterrent effect on hazardous waste crime. To argue otherwise is to consign criminal prosecution to total passivity.

As we come to seriously explore the potential power of punitive sanctions, we must not overlook the importance of contemplating progressive sentencing options for those intermediate cases where stern sanctions are less appropriate. One recommendation is the use of "day fines" to create greater equity between the wealthy and poor offender by correlating offense duration and level of profit derived from the criminal act. We need to dedicate more effort to contemplating the utility of community work orders and restitution payments for certain hazardous waste criminals. The occupational disqualification of corporate executives convicted of hazardous waste offenses could represent a radical, but effective, sanction alternative. The punitive value of this alternative can be high for corporate offenders, as it would prohibit certain career opportunities and prevent corporations from indemnifying the offender through bonuses and benefits. Beyond this, disqualification could help alter corporate norms on criminal activity and serve as a viable alternative to those more traditional sanctions that may fall short in their deterrent impact.

Imaginative Treatment/Reduction Methods

By now, it should be readily clear that the thought of controlling hazardous waste crime exclusively through even the most proficient law enforcement program is naive at best. It is essential that enforcement efforts be supported by the establishment of resourceful new methods for treating and reducing hazardous wastes. We should be asking ourselves not only if we can be more aggressive in siting facilities that practice proven methods, but also if we can achieve major gains in discovering inventive new options for legitimate treatment/reduction.

To make real progress in this area, we have to embark upon the creation of sound hazardous waste problem-assessment and problem solving research strategies. Responsible research programs here will help to explain the logistics of past disposal activities and current generation patterns, and allow us to make accurate future generation estimates. Problem-assessment methods would include archival studies of records of past treatment trends, field and laboratory studies, and an exhaustive analysis of emerging methods. The success of such research would depend upon the ability to measure quantitatively the presence, movement, and ultimate fate of existing hazardous wastes to ascertain resource monitoring needs. Continued research would analyze which methods are currently most effective and how knowledge of the most salient elements of these methods can evolve into new, more constructive means of treatment. Practical research strategies like those above have already led to the discovery of effective treatment alternatives. Such technologies include molten-salt combustion, which uses a pool of molten salts to permit the combustion of hazardous substances below normal ignition levels, and UV/oxidant processes which use either ozone or peroxide for treatment. Two other promising treatment technologies are the plasma-arc process, which uses microwaves to assist in the oxidation of organics in the presence of oxygen at low pressures, and the beta-beam treatment of toxic organics.

One of the most exciting technological breakthroughs since the initial publication of *Dangerous Ground* has been the isolation of natural bacteria and the invention of microbes that break down hazardous wastes. More research is needed in this area but, so far, scientists have been successful in breaking down parathion, a pesticide, and pentachlorophenol, a wood preservative. The problem is that the natural and man-made microbes cannot yet be applied on a wholesale basis, for they can only degrade limited types of hazardous wastes. Nevertheless, this is obviously just the beginning of what should prove to be a wellspring for other microbe-based treatment technologies that are more versatile in their degradation capabilities.

As we promote the study of new treatment alternatives, we should not minimize the value of new strategies that reduce wastes at their source. If we are truly to complement effective enforcement with improved scientific advances, we must convince waste-generating companies to accept the relatively new idea of waste reduction. The trick is to get waste generators to buy into this idea. It can be a costly undertaking, but has been known to pay financial dividends to companies practicing effective reduction methods. Unfortunately, the prospect of saving money through waste reduction techniques does not seem to be enough to persuade industries to implement these methods routinely. Strong economic incentives are needed at the local level to induce waste generators to comply with waste-reduction objectives. As an incentive option, taxes can be assessed on wastes generated using a flat tax (payment unaffected by waste-stream amount), a progressive tax (payment based on waste amount produced per year), or a graduated tax (payment based on the determined level of dangerousness of the generated wastes). Tax breaks could also be employed in the form of credits, deductions, or exemptions based on the amounts of funds dedicated to waste reduction equipment by generators. As a supportive tool, government funds could be directed to waste generator research and development programs exploring new waste-reduction technologies.

These suggestions on new treatment and waste-reduction strategies tap only a small portion of what can be accomplished outside the realm of the criminal justice system to augment environmental enforcement efficacy. Without new treatment/reduction alternatives, law enforcers would be destined to march toward a plainly unrealistic objective: control of hazardous waste crime in a world of rapidly expanding waste streams and shrinking outlets. This, however, should not be interpreted as a signal to let up on law enforcement pressure, for the greatest disincentive to the exploration and discovery of new technologies is the ease with which one may illegally dispose and escape punishment.

Enhancing Intergovernmental Cooperation

If we are truly to overcome the hazardous waste hot-potato mentality, we must go beyond devising more realistic forms of offender sanctions or creating sophisticated substitutes for existing treatment/reduction methods. Our job is not complete unless we position those reforms in the context of the level of ability of government adequately to execute them. We must realize that some of these law enforcement and treatment/reduction goals might be more reasonably attained if they were to be addressed by regional, goal-driven coalitions of governments and government agencies rather than by traditional authorities. Such regional entities might be better equipped to triumph over provincial interests, which frequently undermine attempts at hazardous waste reform. The signs are that many states will be unable to prevail over the backlash of special interest groups and municipal government leaders set against facility siting or will otherwise be prevented from siting because of the incompatibility of states' natural environments with such sites (for example, threats of ground water contamination in states depending on underground aquifers for potable water, and threats to public safety in densely populated states).

Regional approaches to hazardous waste criminal enforcement reform also seem to be gaining some favor. State and local governments agree that effective enforcement cannot be achieved on a state and local level unless state laws are regionally consistent and unless intelligence on criminal activity can be freely exchanged across state borders. The example set by the original Northeast Hazardous Waste Project (now known as the Northeast Environmental Enforcement Project – NEEP) has been followed in all parts of the United States where state governments realize they need contiguous state cooperation to break the pattern of interstate hazardous waste/waste-oil crime. The original members of NEEP included the attorneys general of eleven states (Connecticut, Delaware, Maine, Maryland, Massachusetts, New Hampshire, New Jersey, New York, Pennsylvania, Rhode Island, and Vermont) and was designed to respond to a greater need for interstate cooperation among environmental enforcement officials in the northeast region. The original membership has since expanded to include Ohio, Virginia, West Virginia, and the District of Columbia as full members; and the Province of Quebec, the Defense Criminal Investigative Service, the Naval Criminal Investigative Service, the Air Force Office of Special Investigations, and Environment Canada as associate members.

NEEP has served as the model for the development of three other regional environmental enforcement associations. They are, the Midwest Environmental Enforcement Association, the Southern Environmental Enforcement Network, and the Western States Project—each distinctive in their composition, but dedicated to the same goals and objectives, resulting in a national environmental network. Today forty-seven states, the District of Columbia, and four Canadian provinces are members of at least one regional association dedicated to enhanced environmental crime enforcement at the state level. Membership is composed of representatives from agencies responsible for environmental regulatory activities, civil and administrative enforcement, and criminal investigation and prosecution. These regional associations provide discipline-specific training, general information conferences, networking opportunities, and information and support services. (New Jersey Division of Criminal Justice, 2014, Regional Associations Information Network, 2014).

Finally, to help see that international hazardous waste crime does not fall between the cracks, every responsible national government must demonstrate an open-door policy on communications and cooperation with other national governments. We should increase efforts to apply criminal sanctions within the framework of international law to control hazardous waste violations. This is necessary because these pollutants recognize no jurisdictional boundaries and therefore constitute a danger to people in all countries. Organizations like the United Nations must be at the forefront of movements to develop substantive plans for an enforcement system that closes off opportunities for international hazardous waste disposal crimes. Lately, the United Nations has shown stronger signs that it will be more active on the international front with regard to environmental crime. Through the United Nations Interregional Crime and Justice Research Institute (UNICRI), the UN has bolstered its initiative against the illegal trade and disposal of electronic waste. It has joined INTERPOL in this initiative, along with the Cross-Border Research Association (CBRA) and the Waste of Electrical and Electronic Equipment Forum to form the Countering WEEE Illegal Trade (CWIT) project, funded by the European Community's Seventh Framework Programme. Primary objectives are to estimate the volume of e-waste generated in Europe, assess the type of companies involved in exporting WEEE and analyze the involvement of organized criminal groups and the types of crime associated with illegal trade in WEEE. In addition, the UN has been convening international conferences to address current and emerging threats posed by environmental crime, highlighting its links with organized criminal networks and other crimes of serious nature, with a specific focus on illegal trafficking of e-waste. The conferences are dedicated to the analysis of existing legal issues which permit these crimes to continue largely without prosecution.

As with local and national issues relating to hazardous waste crime, enforcement is no panacea. Incentives must also be cultivated for major industries, especially in densely populated areas of Europe, to support programs for the significant reduction of hazardous waste at its source. The Worldwatch Institute has argued for imposition of "green taxes" to limit waste-generation practices of major industries. Worldwatch recommends environmental taxes modeled after the 1987 Montreal Protocol Treaty, which is aimed at the threat that directly affects us, all-those chemicals that erode the ozone layer. Such a "green tax" reform program is designed to capitalize on existing international agreements that share economic burdens between countries. The goal of control of the international hazardous waste problem is a weighty one and will certainly not be reached overnight. But it is vital if we are to triumph over past complacency on the illegitimate and legitimate norms of hazardous waste shuffling from one caretaker to another.

An encouraging sign that optimized international cooperation is on the horizon is represented by the first Executive Level Environmental Compliance and Enforcement Committee (ECEC) conference co-hosted by the United Nations Environmental Programme and INTERPOL in Nairobi, Kenya in late 2013. The goal of the conference was to design a joint international strategy to tackle environmental crime. For the first time, senior law enforcement officials and representatives from non-governmental organizations, academia and the private sector gathered to strategize on how to best deal with environmental crime in all its forms, and ensure that governments and law enforcement work together to raise awareness of the dangers of environmental crime. Two of the primary topics were cooperation between inter-governmental organizations (IGOs) and environmental enforcement actions.

In his affirmative statement at the conference, Jean-Michel Louboutin, executive director of police services at INTERPOL, aptly characterized the danger environmental crime poses to nations across the globe, and the need for multi-disciplinary, multi-law enforcement agency and multi-national cooperation to take a bold new path to control and deter such crimes in the future.

> Environmental crime worldwide in all its forms represents a serious threat to the world's global security, ecosystems and economy. It represents one of the fastest-growing crime areas, fanned by expanding crime networks, profits, and weak criminal penalties. The fight against environmental crime must involve collective efforts by law enforcement, governments, international organizations and the private sector. INTERPOL will continue to undertake operations in our member countries involving all stakeholders, so as to build capacity, support investigations and reinforce our collective ability to stem such crimes which have a global impact. Maintaining and enhancing environmental security requires a multi-disciplinary response, bringing together science, sustainable development, conservation management, legislators and enforcement (Louboutin, Nov. 6, 2013, 1).

The goal of control of the international hazardous waste problem is a weighty one and will certainly not be reached overnight. But it is vital if we are to triumph over past complacency on the illegitimate and legitimate norms of hazardous waste shuffling from one caretaker to another.

A holistic approach to hazardous waste control on all government levels begins with strong enforcement and treatment/reduction programs at the local and state government levels. But this endeavor will fail unless national governments follow suit. The main barrier to this strategy is a resistance to changing old ideas on the responsibilities of government and the low value placed on intergovernmental initiatives. Elected officials must be less rigid on how they allow government structure to dictate environmental policy decision making and more open to creative thought on how government structure can be molded to adapt to identified hazardous waste control problems. For the holistic approach to prevail, we must permit the higher order of environmental protection to determine the organizational makeups of enforcement/regulatory agencies that may be, in their present state, ill-suited to the task. As put by Volker Meinberg, of the Max Planck Institute for Foreign and International Penal Laws, the time is now for these changes to take place.

> The public's faith in government power in establishing and maintaining environmental order is severely shaken. At a time which requires a considerable degree of individual solidarity in the vital pursuit of environmental preservation, the state bodies ought to be obliged to stand up for a concept of "superior ecological reason" with all their might. . . . The degree of organizational effort required would be considerable; moreover, the agencies involved would have to co-operate in a more flexible manner at all levels, abandoning traditional positions in the interest of a common concern. And last not least, each official would need to be aware of his share of responsibility and act accordingly to the best of his abilities (Meinberg et al. 1989, 65–66).

Appendix A

Organized Crime and Hazardous Waste

Organized Crime Connections: The Controversy

The sense of uncertainty among law enforcement personnel concerning hazardous waste-organized crime connections is typified by Epstein et al.'s (Edwin Stier, 1982) description of their encounter with a top New Jersey government official. The director of New Jersey's Division of Criminal Justice of the attorney general's office, Edwin Stier reported that the major criminal element of hazardous waste offenses appeared not to be organized but was "peripherally" influenced by organized crime members. This statement was made in January 1980. By the fall of 1980, Stier had changed this position when he declared that organized crime was more involved than had been previously assessed.

Based on their interviews with Stier and other law enforcement officials, Epstein et al. (1982) were unable to draw a solid conclusion to the question of organized crime influence. "Is organized crime behind the illegal dumping industry? No one knows for sure. Organized crime has been closely tied to the garbage-hauling industry, especially in the Northeast. It has been further suggested that some hazardous waste operations are syndicate fronts" (166). Some have concluded that hazardous waste crime is dominated by syndicate crime, involving the corruption of public officials, threats, violence, and the defrauding of major corporations. Blumenthal (5 June 1983) portrays the hazardous waste disposal industry in the New York–New Jersey region as a monopolistic customer allocation system in which customers of disposal companies become "property rights" of a particular company at the whim of the company. According to Blumenthal, the system is maintained by the threat of mob violence to dissuade customers from leaving their "rightful" disposal companies.

According to Blumenthal, the chemical waste disposal business emerged as a derivative of the solid waste industry and, consequently, imported the domination of syndicate crime. This reasoning was largely based on the testimony of a former hazardous waste offender, Harold Kaufman, who is now a protected federal witness (Blumenthal, 5 June 1983; *Organized Crime and Hazardous Waste Disposal* 1980).

In his testimony before the House Subcommittee on Oversight and Investigations, Kaufman describes the alleged customer allocation system under which the solid and toxic waste industries are said to operate in New York and New Jersey. Kaufman states that the New Jersey Trade Waste Association, a waste haulers' association, was controlled by organized crime—possibly by the Carl Gambino crime family of Brooklyn, New York. He divulges that after the imposition of a New Jersey hazardous waste manifest checking system in 1978, independent midnight dumpers searched for covers or fronts to hide their illegal operations and found these fronts through association with organized crime. But Kaufman does not apply the concept of customer allocation to other sections of the country nor does he apply it to all of New Jersey. On the subject of customer allocation, he responds in the following manner to subcommittee member James Florio of New Jersey:

> Mr. Florio: We haven't determined, I don't think, that it has actually taken place in a formalized way in the hazard waste industry but I think you have implied—I see you shaking your head yes—that it has started to take place.
>
> Mr. Kaufman: I didn't mean to shake my head that way. I was agreeing with you. I can't speak about the entire toxic waste industry. It's a big industry. I can't speak about the toxic waste industry in Burlington County in New Jersey. For all I know, they may have the most legitimate landfills in the world. (*Organized Crime and Hazardous Waste Disposal* 29)

In 1983, Congress held follow-up hearings on the topic of hazardous waste-organized crime connections. In these hearings, Alan Block of the University of Delaware and Jeremiah McKenna, counsel to the New York State Select Committee on Crime, were introduced as witnesses who would demonstrate the hold of organized crime on the hazard waste industry. Once again, this influence was portrayed as an offshoot of organized crime's control of the solid waste industry.

Block's testimony draws some conclusions from several case studies of solid and hazardous waste firms and their connection to criminality and organized crime, mainly in regard to common, organized crime individuals who figure heavily in these cases.

> It is an industry in which organized crime not only establishes the parameters within which business is conducted, but one in which organized crime adjudicates disputes through its customary methods of intimidation and violence.... By controlling the major trade associations, the primary trade unions, major waste firms, and landfills all with the help of friends in political and criminal justice positions, organized crime is effectively the waste industry. And it may not matter very much whether one is talking about solid or toxic waste. (*Profile of Organized Crime: Mid-Atlantic Region* 1983, 236)

McKenna's testimony distinguishes organized crime as so pervasive that even waste cleanup agencies have been infiltrated. He further remarked that there is evidence that environmental agencies have unwittingly hired these agencies to decontaminate toxic dumps they have created (*Profile of Organized Crime: Mid-Atlantic Region,* 1983).

Both the 1980 and 1983 Congressional hearings highlight judgments on the connections of organized crime to toxic waste disposal crimes in New Jersey and New York. However, the extent of organized crime dominance in hazardous waste offenses in other U.S. regions is not addressed. Some of the purported relations between organized crime and the hazardous waste disposal industry are presented in the testimonies with great specificity while others are quite vague. During hearings held in the interim between the 1980 and 1983 sessions, the credibility of some testimonies was challenged by subcommittee members, in particular that of Harold Kaufman (*Organized Crime Links to the Waste Disposal Industry* 1981).

As part of the 1980 hearings, then New Jersey Attorney General John Degnan cautioned against any premature closure on characterizing all toxic waste crime as operating under the control of organized crime.

> While attention to organized crime is important and demands the serious attention it has received here this morning, to focus on organized crime to the exclusion of other components of the illegal disposal of "toxic wastes" would be misleading and counterproductive. Too often we reach for the simple solution.

> To analyze this critical problem in terms of organized crime alone would be sensational but simplistic, and it would—intentionally or not—serve the interests of an industry which would like nothing better than to have the public's attention diverted from its own failure—historically and contemptuously—to shoulder its social responsibilities. (*Organized Crime and Hazardous Waste Disposal* 89)

Congressional subcommittee hearings on hazardous waste–organized crime links have raised some doubt as to any strong influence. As part of these hearings, the subcommittee released the results of a 1983 survey of 50 state attorneys general that unearthed little "traditional" organized crime involvement. Only 58 of the 1,527 cases were reported to involve organized crime; 11 were in Pennsylvania, 10 were in New Jersey, and 10 were in Ohio. Thirty-four states responded to the survey by disclosing that they had no reports on organized crime involvement in hazardous waste disposal (Cohen, 2 February 1984).

The survey findings were refuted at the hearings by Steven Madonna, currently New Jersey's State Environmental Prosecutor, who pronounced the results spurious because of inadequate law enforcement efforts in many states to detect evidence of organized crime involvement. But when questioned further about the supposed domination in New Jersey, Madonna admitted that he could not state with assurance that organized crime controls the hazardous waste industry in New Jersey or even influences it (Cohen, 2 February 1984).

Repeated inquiries have obviously been unsuccessful in resolving the question of hazardous waste–organized crime connections. Indeed, one becomes wary of the level of confidence expressed by law enforcement and governmental officials indicting the disposal industry at one point and often wavering on such allegations at another. Via congressional hearings, the public has been alerted to signals of the domination of the hazardous waste disposal industry by organized crime only to see these insinuations amended at a later date.

The ongoing controversy has prompted inquiries probing more deeply than to answer the question of the presence or absence of organized crime. First, if the industry is truly manipulated by organized crime, is it due to an importation from the solid waste industry? Second, how valid is the allegation that organized crime operates a customer allocation system within the hazardous waste disposal industry, assuring at least a degree of control? Third, how closely does any organized crime influence come to Hagan's conception of *highly organized crime*?

Organized Crime Connections to Legitimate and Illegitimate Markets: Empirical Research

There exists a meager amount of empirical research on organized crime's influence on the hazardous waste industry. Nevertheless, one should not overlook several studies of organized crime's association with both legitimate and illegitimate markets, especially in reference to the operational trends of organized crime within these markets.

Two works by Peter Reuter figure significantly in spelling out organized crime's role in illegitimate and legitimate markets. Reuter's study on the underworld of illegal gambling and loan sharking (1983) evolved into an analysis of the organization and principles underlying illegal markets generally. The results of his study explode the myth that the Mafia's "visible hand" of violence and corruption is the dominant force behind these markets.

Reuter's data were collected from New York police department wiretap applications and search warrant requests,[1] arrest reports, confiscated records of numbers banks and bookmaking operations, interview's with police and prosecutors, and interviews with seven professional informants. Areas of data collection concentrated on types of criminal roles played, transactions between actors, territorial divisions of the illegal markets, gross profits, degree of cheating, and use of extortion and physical violence (Reuter 1983, 6–13).

The major objective of the study became the testing of the doctrine of the 1950s Kefauver Committee, from which sprouted the now commonly held belief that numbers and bookmaking are controlled by the Mafia and criminal groups that have interests in other criminal activities. Reuter approached this issue from an industrial-organization perspective by collecting data bearing on the structure and conduct[2] of these markets to test the assertion that the numbers and bookmaking markets do not function like competitive markets (Reuter 1983 177–187).

Reuter's results indicate that numbers banks are modest-sized operations yielding a substantial, but variable, income for the banker. Reuter concludes that these findings do not justify the claim that numbers provide the stable source of capital accumulation for the growth of large-scale, multiple-enterprise, criminal empires. The belief that the numbers business is a controlled activity is further debunked by the evidenced level of competition by "collectors" and "controllers." Reuter did not find evidence to support the claim that Mafia members are involved in numbers, but rather found that they play no part in controlling entry on prices in the markets (Reuter 1983 153–173).

It was uncovered that Mafia members are active only as bettors and financiers in the area of bookmaking. In addition, since bookmakers borrow from sources other than the Mafia, there is little Mafia control exerted over the business. The study characterizes the world of bookmakers as experiencing low profit margins and common, long-term financial difficulties. The unpredictable loyalties of their "runners" (retailers) often lead to unmet profit expectations (Reuter 1983, 167–168).

Of greater relevance to the present study is Reuter's case study with Rubenstein and Wynn (1983). It is a rigorous follow-up to Reuter's preliminary foray (1982) into racketeering in the solid waste collection business. The study drew on information sources such as the public record, law enforcement agency files, investigatory reports, and informant evidence. The authors claim that theirs is the first attempt to study a legitimate industry in which racketeers have been alleged to play a dominant role and that the study challenges beliefs about the sources and consequences of racketeer involvement in legitimate businesses.

The authors adopt the definition of racketeering set out by the *National Advisory Commission on Criminal Standards and Goals* (1978, 7–8 and 213–215): a continuing criminal conspiracy in which the objects of the conspiracy are to be attained through the use of force, fraud, or corruption. Whenever racketeers wish to become a directing force of a legitimate industry, the authors argue, they will seek to organize a specific type of cartel (previously explained as a customer allocation agreement):

> Here the principal cartel rule will be that each customer belongs to a particular cartel member; others cannot compete for the allocated customer's business. The cartel is unlikely to attempt to control member prices. This conclusion comes from consideration of the cost of detecting and sanctioning violations of other kinds of agreements, the probability of an effective prosecution of various agreements and the attractiveness of the simplest possible rule for an illegal cartel. (7)

The authors add that customer allocation can be employed only where the location of the customer population is fixed and the service is delivered to the customer. The evidence of customer allocation is seen as less efficient production (since lower costs will not translate into greater market share because of customer allocation), higher prices (the result of imposed competition restraints), and small firms. The authors also believe that the reputation for racketeer involvement is a barrier to entering the industry.

The researchers used New York City and a state identified only as "Victoria" for their case studies. They found in New York City direct evidence of the existence of a customer allocation agreement. Documented hearings of the Department of Consumer Affairs indicated that the purchase of a customer by one cartel from another gave the purchaser the exclusive right to service that customer. Also, it was found that cartels routinely sell groups of customers to each other and as the customer allocation process solidifies threats of entry by new cartels are lessened.

The most active role played by racketeers in these customer allocation agreements was found to be that of assisting in the mediation of inevitable allocation disputes. It was found that the central role of racketeers as mediators of disputes over the assignments of particular customers applied in "Victoria" as well, though the participation there was less direct (9–13).

In short, Reuter et al.'s study of the solid waste industry arrived at several meaningful findings:

- The two areas studied demonstrated the importance of criminal conspiracies in which force and coercion are used.
- Those who benefit most from these conspiracies do not, themselves, have a law enforcement reputation as racketeers.
- While racketeers play major roles in these conspiracies, they do not control or dominate the participants in the business, but perform certain services to the industry. In general, they assist in the enforcement and continuation of conspiracies that they originally instigated. (3)

The authors discovered that the racketeers allied themselves with corrupt unions to form anticompetitive cartels that yield profits for the industry close to those that could be obtained through a monopoly. They concluded that such events would not occur in industries controlled by large corporations or involving high technology but rather in small, family-based enterprises like the solid waste industry. The authors also concluded that there is little justification for assertions by law enforcement and the media of racketeer domination and that these assertions have served to discourage outsiders from entering the business, thus helping entrench racketeer influence in the industry (v–vi).

The studies thus far described examine organized crime's connection to specified markets by blending interviews of offenders and enforcement personnel and archival case research. Any serious effort to quantify the level of organized crime along the lines of Hagan's continuum is absent from these studies. Yet the analysis by Reuter et al. has some potentially profound implications for the present study in that the results establish that organized crime may influence the solid waste industry in a marginal manner, but display absolutely no confirmation of its being a dominating force. This conclusion casts suspicion on the validity of the theory that the solid waste industry has exported organized crime domination to the hazardous waste industry.

Reuter has assailed the orthodox position on organized crime, emanating from the Kefauver Committee's conclusions, for encouraging media distortions of the "visible hand" of organized crime as being the driving force of much professional economic crime. Neither Reuter's gambling and loan sharking study nor his collaborative study with Rubenstein and Wynn on the solid waste industry support the Kefauver conjectures.

The vacuum of works on hazardous waste crime and organized crime was partially filled in 1983 and 1985 by an article and a book coauthored by Alan Block and Frank Scarpitti. The two works assert that hazardous waste crime, especially in highly industrialized states, is controlled and directed by organized crime syndicates. In their 1983 piece, the authors go so far as to judge any other interpretation of the phenomenon as entirely unacceptable.

We argue that the hazardous waste industry is not just partly made up of career criminals, but that its structure is determined by organized crime syndicates. Therefore, we find that the characterization of the problems associated with the illegal disposal of hazardous waste as a variant or type of white-collar crime to be incorrect, perhaps even insidious. (104)

In *Poisoning for Profit: The Mafia and Toxic Waste In America*, published in 1985, the authors take an even more passionate position on the topic of organized crime domination. Early in the book, they describe organized crime as that dubbed "Mafia" or "Cosa Nostra" by law enforcement but waver on any consistent definition throughout the book. They also include waste generators, who contract with syndicate crime–infiltrated treatment facilities, in their conception of organized criminals. They allege that the degree of organized crime infiltration in the northeastern United States has been underestimated, as has been the importation of such infiltration from the solid waste handling industry. Although they admit to some speculation here, the authors contend that the grip of organized crime is no looser in the western United States. They blame ineffective enforcement and political corruption for the overall thriving of organized crime in the hazardous waste industry.

The 1985 book has stirred much controversy and has led to several lawsuits against the authors and publisher, a journalist's repudiating of his own dust-cover endorsement, and reviews critical of the lack of objectivity and the lack of citations to information sources (Blumenthal, 10 February 1985). According to what little is reported by the authors regarding their methods of research, their conclusions are based primarily on the interviews of several municipal police officers, a state police detective, and two former offenders (one a federal informant), and the gleaning of newspaper articles. At the center of the book are charges lodged by the police officers against superiors and state officials suggesting enforcement incompetence and corruption; the charges are unconfirmed.

While the work suffers from a lack of rigor in data collection and analysis, it highlights the difficulty of meaningful research in this area, largely the result of prohibited access to desirable data. Generalizations based on disputable data sources can force a premature and unsound position on an issue such as the hazardous waste crime–organized crime question. Block and Scarpitti's work, at least, forces us to keep looking for the right answers to their valuable questions.

Notes

1. These data proved to be helpful in detailing work routines and role interactions within gambling operations.
2. Reuter defined structure as the number of sellers, the percentage of the market supplied by the largest producers, the presence or absence of barriers to entry, and geographic dispersion of sellers and buyers. Conduct was explained as pricing policies and coordination among sellers.

Appendix B

Research Methods

A contextual approach to a social phenomenon assumes that the phenomenon is in some way unique or exceptional and that it can be aptly explained only in the context of its social medium.

The primary research goal of the collection and analysis of data for this study is to effect a contextual analysis of the hazardous waste offense/offender and, in doing so, afford a holistic appreciation of this phenomenon.

Sources of Data

The contextual analysis of the hazardous waste offense/offender study uses a research design that combines archival content analysis with interview surveys. The content analysis was conducted on case files of disposed hazardous waste offense. The study also obtained information from interviews with state law enforcement personnel specializing in hazardous waste offenses. The data are supplemented by case file transcripts of investigator/prosecutor interviews of offenders, particularly with regard to methods of offense commission and detection-avoidance techniques.

The study sample was drawn from all disposed hazardous waste offense cases[1], from January 1, 1977, to January 1, 1985, from the attorney general offices of New Jersey, Pennsylvania, Maryland, and Maine. The three-MidAtlantic states and one New England state were chosen for three chief reasons. First three of these states have exhibited the greatest concentration of known hazardous waste offenses in the United States and, second, all four have displayed some of the most earnest systematic efforts in the United States to control these offenses via state-level enforcement agencies. They therefore represent the best available material on hazardous waste offenses within the context of vigorous enforcement. Finally, the three contiguous states were able to furnish data on any criminal networks that demonstrate evidence of operating beyond state borders.

Contents of Files

The general file contents for each state were similar, with slight variations in document formats. Case files contained: (1) investigative memoranda leading to the opening of the case; (2) investigative memoranda tracing both pre- and post-arrest case progress; (3) investigative interviews with informants, coworkers, and associates of offenders; (4) surveillance reports: (5) transcripts of undercover tape recordings of offenders; (6) transcripts of grand jury witness testimonies; (7) arrest/indictment documents; and (8) "judgment of conviction" forms.

Each of the eight general categories of documents yielded high-quality information pertinent to the study's research questions. Overall, investigative memoranda became the primary source of clarifying characteristics of the offense event. When arranged sequentially, the documents aptly chronicled characteristics such as (1) means of discovery; (2) methods of surveillance; (3) methods of disposal; (4) place of disposal; and (5) types of materials disposed. Investigative memoranda was also enlightening on subjects like conspiracies within companies or with outsiders, organized crime connections, and connections to other hazardous waste cases.

Transcripts of conversations and testimonies of offenders and their associates were especially useful in explaining commission and detection-avoidance methods and the structure of criminal conspiracies. In cases where syndicate crime family connections were apparent, these transcripts sometimes presented textured descriptions of events and situations leading to these connections, specifics on the syndicate crime families involved, plus the types of services rendered by these crime families.

Other official system-process documents (for example, arrest/indictment forms, judgment of conviction forms) contained data related to offender background data and to charging and sentencing procedures. This information included past arrest records, occupational histories, organizational levels of offenders, charges/counts, types of pleas, plea agreement terms, sentences, and judicial rationale for the imposition of the sentences.

For several areas, case file data were complemented through other archival sources. For the examination of syndicate crime connections, special data were gleaned from intelligence reports from the New Jersey State Police and the New Jersey Division of Criminal Justice. To reaffirm that case files were comprehensive in their information on offenders' criminal histories, state police criminal background checks of offenders were employed for each of the sample states. In New Jersey, quarterly reports of the New Jersey Environmental Prosecutions Unit were also consulted. Much of the data found here duplicated data retrieved from case files; some material was helpful in answering questions on innovations in investigative techniques.

Interview Questionnaires

The decision was made to employ open- instead of closed-ended interview questions, with attention to conclusions drawn by Shuman and Presser's experiments on questionnaire form, wording, and context (1981). Their experiments dispel some of the age-old presumptions of the superiority of open-ended questions regarding salience of responses, the avoidance of social desirability, and a prevention of mechanical choice and/or guessing. They conclude, through the administration of open-ended and closed-ended versions of work-value questionnaires, that open-ended formats generally suffer from vagueness of expression by respondents and interviewer failure to probe adequately. They conclude that the disadvantages of closed-ended questionnaires are minimized especially when surveying respondents educated in the field of study. However, they are confident that an open-ended format is adaptable to subject areas of newly emergent phenomena, and when this phenomena is in the midst of rapidly changing conditions—both of which conditions apply to the subject of this study. "Open interview responses take on increasing value because they allow future scientists to create in retrospect new categories undreamt of by the original investigators—to put, in effect, new questions to one's predecessor's respondents" (111).

The questionnaire surveys were divided into five areas: (1) offense structure, (2) offender methods and skills, (3) controls/influences on the offender, (4) criminal networks, and (5) investigative/prosecutorial methods. In keeping with Gibbs and Shelley's study of commercial thieves (1981), the flexibility of the interview's application was stressed to complement the exploratory nature of the study. In effect, the questionnaire served as more of an interview guide as opposed to an interview schedule. The printed questions acted as starting points that often evolved into other questions on related subjects not originally considered. (For example, the discovery of the role of medical research on hospital wastes in Maryland led to unanticipated questions on the causes of this problem and methods of control.) Especially with regard to criminal networks and significant outsiders, questions answered by some respondents prompted a revision of questions posed to subsequent interview subjects.

The questionnaire's first section, "Offense Structure," centers on the study areas of organized crime, professional crime, and criminal networks. Questions 1, 2, and 5 attempt to gauge the continuum level of organized crime experienced in hazardous waste crime cases. Question 3 tries to determine the extent of the offenders' assimilation into their profession. In essence, the question here is: Do they engage in self-imposed isolation from legitimate industry operatives, or do they function freely within the industry as they pursue their criminal trade? Question 4 elicits input on how offenders might shape the legal environment through an interplay with public officials, how these officials act as significant outsiders, and how they network with other offenders. The sixth and final question has a dual purpose. It probes the topic of customer allocation by ascertaining the extent to which employers within the monopolized solid waste industry have entered the hazardous waste arena. It also seeks to determine the prevalence of environmental offense histories of offenders.

Question 1 of the second section, "Offender Methods and Skills," is posed not only to ascertain how the crimes are engineered but how their form may have changed, over time, in reaction to enforcement improvement. Question 2 is a measure of the respondents' impressions on the level of expertise required to commit the offenses. Sophisticated technical skills here could indicate a certain professionalism needed for commission success. The third question, on the absence of treatment apparatus at offending "treatment" facilities, helps us to understand the preplanned criminal intent of offenders.

The "Controls/Influence on Offenders" section is primarily concerned with the perceived severity of legal controls (regulatory laws, criminal laws) imposed on offenders and their variations among states, and any conflict with local ordinances the sudden imposition of these laws might cause. Also, the section raises the issue of possible management and/or coworker coercion of workers to be criminal participants—an assessment of the "grid" and "group" dimensions in the hazardous waste work place.

Data Collection Strategies

The study's units of observation are hazardous waste incidents subject to formal criminal prosecution in the four indicated states, as well as offenders within these cases. Within case files, all documentations of case processing, offense events, offender communications, and enforcement efforts were examined. Offense and offender characteristics act as units of analysis and include patterns of offenses, tactics of social control–avoidance, and criminal decision making. The study treats criminal cases as social artifacts in that it investigates the social interactions between different types of hazardous waste offenders, and also the interactions between those offenders and enforcers.

The following is a general outline of study methods:

- *Preliminary Examination of Case Files.* A small sample of hazardous waste offense cases was selected from the Hazardous Waste Prosecutions Section of the New Jersey attorney general's Division of Criminal Justice to determine the most feasible and economical methods of collecting the prepared data and noting the types of case documents that would yield the most complete information. During this phase a data-collection instrument was developed for use in collecting documented data from case files constituting the sample.
- *Creation of Questionnaire Instrument.* The results of the preliminary examination of offense files were used to shape the questions and format of the questionnaire in regard to open- or close-endedness.
- *Instrument Pretest.* This was achieved by conducting questionnaire interviews with the investigators and prosecution attorneys who had worked on the sampled cases. The pretest collected interview data that demonstrated the extent to which unavailable case file data could be collected through interviews. That is, it uncovered information relevant to a comprehensive analysis that did not always appear in file documentations. In addition, these interview data were checked against comparable case file data to verify reliability. Both the questionnaire interview instrument and case content analysis instrument were revised according to findings of the pretest.
- *Study Site Collection.* After the pretesting process was completed, case file data were recorded at each site. That process was followed by the administration of the survey interview instrument to those investigators and prosecutors identified during the case file review stage.

Research Analysis

Questionnaire Interviews

Interview questions have been guided by previously articulated hazardous waste crime issues reported by other authors (Blumenthal, 5 June 1983; Epstein et al. 1982; Krajick 1981; Wolf 1983) and by the theoretical motivations of the study. The basic open-endedness of many of the questions allowed for a recognition of pertinent subjects that the prospectus had not considered and allowed for the effective analysis of common themes within responses.

Content Analysis

The study's method of archival research is, in a pure sense, inductive, in that it begins with observed reality and attempts to find general, regular patterns that correspond to that reality. The initial inventory of case files refined into general categories information derived from investigative and prosecutorial communiques, witness testimonies, pre-sentence reports, as well as other file materials. Close attention was paid to the relative frequency of given content characteristics, such as the number of significant outsiders used, as well as the presence of organized crime contacts.

Much of the archival data collected entailed the recording and coding of "hard" indicators, such as numbers of offenses charged and rates of conviction. But a substantial portion of the archival data was less conspicuous, concealed within narrative passages of witness testimonies and investigative memoranda.

To ensure high levels of reliability and validity, coding schemes were presented on a sample of New Jersey hazardous waste crime case files. Manifest- and latent-content indicators of variable attributes were put into operation and used in the coding of several units of observation. Results were reviewed to take special note of those observations not easily classified with the objective of the refinement of operational definitions.

Threats to Validity

Interviews

Initial concerns as to threats to the validity of interviews were, first, the extent of hazardous waste crime experiences of the potential interviewees and, second, the maturity of their interpretations of experience. To ensure that only the most experienced enforcers were interviewed, respective state liaisons were directed to identify durations of task force employment for each investigator and prosecutor and to determine their participation in hazardous waste offenses. Only those with at least one year of task force experience and direct participation in the investigation, surveillance, and/or prosecution of hazardous waste offenses were considered for interviews. No interviewee was required to recall information from further back than six years. Also, when possible, information retrieved in interviews was crosschecked with official case versions to gauge consistency.

Sampling

Studying the total population of disposed hazardous waste offenses within the sample states presents both benefits and drawbacks to the quality of the study. A primary benefit is that studying completed cases supplies a means to examine the criminal event from its initiation as an official crime, via arrest, to its final disposition. This allows us to explore how the informal and formal mechanisms of the law enforcement community shape these crimes (how they force changes in commission methods), the degree of success in prosecutions, common hindrances to success, and the severity of punishment. In short, taking account of the complete case process permits us to account for the full role that the criminal justice system plays in these offenses.

However, certain research drawbacks are inherent in this tack. Concentrating solely on those cases discovered by criminal justice authorities slights those cases committed but not reported and those that are reported but never lead to an arrest. We are presently unable to discern the total volume of undetected hazardous waste criminal events. Any public survey that may come close to naming this number is beyond the parameters of the current study.

In interviews, law enforcement personnel assessed that of the total offenses reported, the percentage of hazardous waste incidents where investigations are made and no evidence of criminality is found is far greater than the percentage of cases where criminality is found but no arrest is made (for example, offender not identified, insufficient evidence to arrest). Interviewees attributed this to the upsurge in public awareness, sparking an increase in citizen, local-enforcement, and business-community reports, many of which prove to be unfounded or not fitting the category of hazardous waste offenses. From a research standpoint this is heartening, for it establishes that the great majority of those cases not encompassed in the study sample have been weeded out by authorities as not warranting criminal charging under current hazardous waste crime statutes. It is nonetheless recognized that the inability to capture data on offenders who are unable to be identified by law enforcement officials has some negative effects on the study's results. Indeed, the possibility exists that these unknown offenders may share certain characteristics or behavior patterns that could strengthen their ability to avoid identification and add greater depth to information presently in this study.

The most obvious potentially harmful threat to external validity was the possibility of misrepresenting characteristics of hazardous waste offenders by relying solely on analyses of those officially processed by the criminal justice system. Interview data are less affected by this threat than are data from files, for the interview data encompass events that may involve those who were known by authorities but not officially charged. However, both data sources suffer from the fact that they yield data on only those offenses that have come to the attention of enforcement authorities and provide little on cases that have not.

The sample is representative of two major categories of offenders: The first comprises those rare, one-event offenders whose unsophisticated and obtrusive actions, due to lack of experience in such criminal ventures, "beg" detection. The second, much larger, and believed to be a truer component of the offender population are those treaters, haulers, and generators targeted by enforcement through records of ongoing regulatory violations and spotlighting of criminal arrangements made by treaters and haulers with generators.

The one criminal occupational area that was originally thought to be underrepresented by the sample was large corporate waste generators that illegally dispose on-site. In chapter 10, "Investigative Methods/ Prosecution Obstacles," interviewees convey their problems with detecting and prosecuting such offenses. Lack of investigative experience in understanding complicated manufacturing processes is one roadblock. Another is the lack of visibility of large generators when they illegally dispose on their generating grounds or other property they may own. Also, many such generators operate in close proximity to other similarly-sized operation that share outlets to sewage systems. In this case, ascertaining the source of illegally disposed hazardous wastes is frequently an impossible task.

Recognizing such enforcement obstacles, and their possible impact on the sample, one should be aware that a primary value of the study is not only to identify known offender characteristics but also to identify those areas where enforcement has not matched the technological sophistication of offenders.

Some of the greater fears of sample misrepresentation were partially dispelled by the findings of a national survey of small generators conducted for the EPA (Abt Associates Inc. 1985). The study's authors base their definition of small generators on the volume of wastes generated per month; those generating less than 1,000 kilograms of hazardous wastes are defined as small generators. The authors found that although small generators make up less than one-half of 1 percent of the total quantity of hazardous waste generated annually, they account for

98 percent of the total number of hazardous waste generators nationally. It should not be surprising, then, that small generators dominate the study's generator sample and that these offenders account for criminal cases involving low waste-volume disposals.

Of the sample of 30 waste-generator offenders, five are Waste-generating corporations with over 1,000 employees. Although these five companies comprise a small portion of the generator sample, their characteristics are indicative of what may be a partially hidden area of hazardous waste crime.

It should be kept in mind that the present study is largely a descriptive one; it sets out to describe criminal behavior, activities, and associations of employees of the waste-generating, transporting, and disposal industries. Like Reuter et al.'s study of crime in the solid waste industry (1983) and Levi's study of professional fraudsters (1981), it focuses solely on the criminal side of a profession. On the subject of hazardous waste crime, the present study identifies patterns of illegality routinely practiced by related corporations and their operatives. The study also provides baseline data useful for the pursuit of other, more intricate and explanatory data on this and other associated topics.

Although this analysis of the characteristics of hazardous waste offenders and their offenses is informative, the use of certain comparison-group data would make it more so. Our ignorance of certain characteristics of the personnel of legitimate hazardous waste handling firms reflects our inability to analyze the industry as a whole. Hence, it is not always possible to conclude that the discovered characteristics of the offender distinguish him from his legitimate industry counterpart. A perfect example of this is in the area of personal and occupational characteristics. Data on offenders' backgrounds of violations were accessible to the study through criminal case file material and state police background checks. Unfortunately, identical data for the hazardous waste industry as a whole were unattainable. Therefore, we still do not know if past records of official hazardous waste industry offenders are significantly different from those in the industry not arrested for hazardous waste offenses. We are still in the dark as to the extent of past regulatory violations of nonoffender personnel and how they compare to known offenders.

Although the lack of a comparison group detracts somewhat from the utility of the study, it should not detract from the value it does possess. For instance, some state legislatures have placed great emphasis on the role of criminal background checks in eliminating those applying for licensing in the hazardous waste treatment field. Study results show a minority of cases where criminal backgrounds were present. The uncovering of this fact may be sobering to those who see such criminal background-based screenings as a panacea for ridding the industry of those apt to dispose illegally. A single examination of offenders' criminal records, along with interview data, can also point out what marginally violative behavior presages the official hazardous waste criminal event.

Note

1.   This entails all nonpending cases in which individuals or corporations were charged with illegal disposing of hazardous wastes, conspiracy to illegally dispose of hazardous wastes, or fraudulent schemes connected with the disposal of hazardous wastes.

References

Abt Associates Inc. (1985). National small quantity hazardous waste generator survey. Washington, DC: Environmental Protection Agency, Office of Solid Waste.

Akerstrom, M. (1985). Crooks and squares: Lifestyles of thieves and addicts in comparison to conventional people. New Brunswick, NJ: Transaction Publishers.

Albanese, J. (1989). *Organized crime in America.* Cincinnati: Anderson Publishing Co.

Albini, J. (1971). *The American Mafia: Genesis of a legend.* New York: Appleton-Century-Crofts.

Associated Press, (1984, August 30). House reports on EPA charges White House still withholds data.

Associated Press, (1989, February 23). Report faults EPA's handling of contracts.

Babbie, E. (1973). *The practice of social research.* Belmont, CA: Wadsworth.

Bardach, E., and R. A. Kagan (1982). *Going by the book: The problem of regulatory unreasonableness.* Philadelphia: Temple University Press.

Bates, T. (1990, June 28). DEP lawyers unhappy with transfer plan. *The Asbury Park Press.*

Bates, T. (1990, August 8). New state standards set for storage tanks. *The Asbury Park Press,* p. A6.

Baumbart, R. (1961). How ethical are businessmen? *Harvard Law Review* 39: 5–176.

Begos, K. (2014, January 5) 4 states confirm water pollution from drilling. *USA Today.*

Berke, R. (1990, April 17). Oratory of environmentalism becomes the sound of politics. *The New York Times,* p. 1.

Bishop, G. (1990, August 5). Ten years later: Final battle at hand in hunt for hazardous waste sites. *The Star Ledger,* p. 1.

Bishop, G. (1990, September 9). Deadline nears for removing carcinogenic PCB's. *The Star Ledger,* p. 12.

Block, A., and F. Scarpitti (1983). Defining illegal hazardous waste disposal: White collar or organized crime. In G. Waldo (ed.), *Career criminals.* Beverly Hills: Sage.

Block, A., and F. Scarpitti, (1985). *Poisoning for profit: The Mafia and toxic waste in America.* New York: William Morrow & Co.

Blumenthal, R. (1983, June 5). Illegal dumping of toxins laid to organized crime. *The New York Times,* pp. 1 and 44.

Blumenthal, R. (1985, February 10). Charges in book on toxic waste called false. *The New York Times*, p. 42.

Brenner, J. K. (1981). Liability for generators of hazardous waste: The failure of existing enforcement mechanisms. *Georgetown Law Journal* 69(4): 1047–1081.

Brenner, S. N., and E. A. Molander, (1977). Is the ethics of business changing? *Harvard Business Review* 55: 59–70.

Britan, G. (1981). Contextual evaluation: An ethnographic approach to program assessment. In R. F. Conner (ed.), *Methodological advances in evaluation research.* Beverly Hills: Sage.

Brownstein, R. (1981). The toxic tragedy. In R. Hader, R. Brownstein, and J. Richard (eds.), *Who's poisoning America: Corporate pollutors and their victims in the chemical age.* San Francisco: Sierra Club Books.

Burns, R., M. Lynch and P Stretesky (2008). *Environmental Law, Crime and Justice.* New York. LFB Scholarly Publishing.

Burroughs, T. (1990, June 25). Environmental lawyers organize to beef up their cause in Jersey. *The Star Ledger*, p. 29.

Burt, R. (1982). *Toward a structural theory of action: Network models of social structure, perceptions and action.* New York: Academic.

Burt, R. (1983). Distinguishing relational contents. In R. Burt & M. Minor (eds.), *Applied network analysis.* Beverly Hills: Sage.

Campbell, D. T., and J. C. Stanley (1963). *Experimental and quasi-experimental designs for research.* Chicago: Rand McNally College Publishing Co.

Carroll, A. (1975). Managerial ethics: A post-Watergate view. *Business Horizons 18:* 75–80.

Carson, R. (1962). *Silent spring.* New York: Houghton Mifflin.

Clinard, M. B. (1979). *Illegal corporate behavior.* Washington, DC: National Institute of Law Enforcement and Criminal Justice.

Clinard, M. B. (1983). *Corporate ethics and crime.* Beverly Hills: Sage.

Clinard, M. B., and P. C. Yeager (1980). *Corporate crime.* New York: The Free Press.

Clinard, M. B., P. C. Yeager, J. Brissette, D. Petrashek, and E. Harries (1979). *Illegal corporate behavior.* Washington, DC: U.S. Department of Justice, Law Enforcement Assistance Administration.

Cohen, A. K. (1977). The concept of criminal organization. *British Journal of Criminology* 17: 97–111.

Cohen, R. (1984, February 2). Jersey lawman faults study of mob-pollution tie. *The Star-Ledger*, p. 7.

Daley, B. (2005, July 24). Maine's most wanted: junkyard polluter: Owner left mess that cost millions. *The Boston Globe.*

Defranco, E. J. (1973). *Anatomy of a scam—A case study of a planned bankruptcy by organized crime.* Washington, DC: U.S. Department of Justice, Law Enforcement Assistance Administration.

Ditton, J. (1977). *Part-time crime: An ethnography of fiddling and pilferage.* London: Macmillan.

Enforcement in the 1990's project (1991). Washington, DC: The Environmental Protection Agency.

Environmental Resources Management Inc. (1985). *New Jersey hazardous waste facilities plan.* Trenton: New Jersey Hazardous Waste Facilities Siting Commission.

Epstein, S., L. Brown, and C. Pope (1982). *Hazardous waste in America.* San Francisco: Sierra Club Books.

Evan, W. M. (1976). *Organization theory: Structure, systems and environments.* New York: John Wiley.

Fromm, S. (1989, November 3). Atlantic coast officials vow to unite on ocean, *The Trenton Times,* p. 1.

Gallagher, A. (1988, May 18). Water pollutors should be sent to prison, environmentalists say. *The Home News.*

Geis, G., and T. R. Clay (1982). Criminal enforcement of California's occupational carcinogens control act. In G. Geis (ed.), *On white collar crime.* Lexington, MA: Lexington Books.

Gibbs. J. J., and P. J. Shelley (1981). Life in the fast lane: A retrospective view by commercial thieves. *Journal of Research in Crime and Delinquency* 19(2): 299–330.

Gould, L., E. Bittner, S. Messinger, F. Powledge, and S. Chaneles (1966). *Crime as a profession.* Washington, DC: U.S. Government Printing Office.

Green, J. (2014, August 26) Don't Waste Our Open Space: 6 charged with illegal dumping on N.J. lands. *South Jersey Times.*

Greenberg, M. R., and R. Anderson (1984). *Hazardous waste sites: The credibility gap.* New Brunswick, NJ: The Center for Urban Policy Research/Rutgers University.

Hagan, R. (1983). the organized crime continuum: A further specification of a new conceptual model. *Criminal Justice Review* 8(2): 52–57.

Henry S. (1978). *The hidden economy: The context and control of borderline crime.* Oxford: Martin Robinson.

Hopkins, A. (1979). The anatomy of corporate crime. In P. R. Wilson and J. Braithwaite (eds.), *Two faces of deviance.* Queensland: Queensland Press.

Inciardi, J. A. (1975). *Careers in crime.* Chicago: Randy McNally.

INTERPOL (2013, October 5). INTERPOL and partners crack down on illegal e-waste trade INTERPOL report. Lyon, France.

Jaffe, H. (1990, March 3). Tracking code permitted hazardous wastes at improper sites. *The Star Ledger,* p. 8.

Johnson, T. (1990, February 25). Special prosecutor targets prevention of ecological crises. *The Star Ledger,* p. 11.

Kates, G. (2014, July 14). Environmental crime: the prosecution gap. The Crime Report.

Katz, J. (2015, February 20). Duke energy is charged in huge coal ash leak. The New York Times.

Klockars, C. B. (1974). *The professional fence.* London: Tavistock.

Knoke, D., and J. Kuklinski (1982). *Network analysis.* Beverly Hills: Sage.

Kobell, R. (2012, December 1). Report says MD is getting lax in fighting environmental crime. *The Bay Journal.* Chesapeake Media Service Lack of resources to handle growing number of cases cited.

Krajick, K. (1981). When will police discover the toxic time bomb? and toxic waste is big business for the mod. *Police Magazine,* May: 6–20.

Kramer, R. (1982). Corporate crime: An organizational perspective. In P. Wickman and T. Daily (eds.), *White collar and economic crime.* Lexington, MA: Lexington Books.

Leary, M. (2015, January 16) Maine's Growing Meth Lab Problem Targeted by Governor, Attorney General. *MPBM News.*

Leavitt, H. (1951). Some effects of communication patterns on group performance. *Journal of Abnormal Psychology* 46; 38–50.

Leepson, M. (1982). Toxic substance control. In *Environmental issues: Prospects and problems.* Washington, DC: Editorial Research Reports.

Letkemann, P. (1973). *Crime as Work.* Englewood Cliffs, NJ: Prentice Hall.

Levi, M. (1981). *The phantom capitalists.* London: Heinneman Educational Books.

Lin, N. (1976). *Foundations of social research.* New York: McGraw Hill.

Lofland, J. (1976). *Doing social life.* Englewood Cliffs, N.J.: Prentice-Hall.

Louboutin, J. (2013, November 6) INTERPOL International Environmental Compliance and Enforcement Conference. United Nations Complex, Nairobi, Kenya.

Lupsha, P. (1983). Networks versus networking: Analysis of an organized crime group. In G. Waldo (ed.), *Career criminals.* Beverly Hills: Sage.

Magnuson, E. (1985). A problem that cannot be buried: The poisoning of America continues, *Time,* 14 October: 76–90.

Mars, G. (1982). *Cheats at work: An anthropology of workplace crime.* London: George Allen & Unwin.

Martens, F. (1985). A counter-response to Scarpitti and Block. *Academy of Criminal Justice Science Newsletter,* September: 4.

McDermott, M. F. (1982). Occupational disqualification of corporate executives—an innovative condition of probation. *Journal of Law and Criminology* 73, 604–641.

McIntosh, M. (1975). *The organization of crime.* London: Macmillan.

McIntosh, M. (1976). Thieves and fences: Markets and power in professional crime. British Journal of Criminology 259–266.

McPheeters, B. (1980). Inactive or abandoned hazardous waste disposal sites: Coping with a costly past. *Southern California Law Review* 53(6).

Meinberg, V., J. Donnen, H. Hoch, and W. Link (1989). Environmental crime—Economic and "everyone's" delinquency. Paper presented at the Max Planck Institute for Foreign and International Penal Law, Freiburg, Germany.

Metz, B. (1985). *No more Mr. nice guy: Hazardous waste enforcement management in the USA.* Groningen, The Netherlands: Ministry of Housing, Physical Planning and Environment, Regional Inspectorate for the Environment.

Mueller, G. O. W. (1979). Offenses against the environment and their prevention: An international appraisal. *Annals* 56.

Miller, S. (1980). Corporate criminal liability: A principal extended to its limits. *Federal Bar Journal* 38, (49–63).

Mitchell, J. C. (1969). The concept and use of social networks. In J. C. Mitchell (ed.), *Social networks in urban situations.* Manchester: Manchester University Press.

Moore, W. (1974). *The Kefauver committee and the politics of crime*. Columbia: U. of Missouri Press.

Mugdan, W. E., and B. R. Adler (1985). The 1984 RCRA amendments: Congress as a regulatory agent. *Columbia Journal of Environmental Law* 10(2): 215–254.

Mullan, W. C. (1975). *Theft and disposition of securities by organized crime*. Huntsville, TX: Sam Houston State University, criminal justice monograph.

Mustokoff, M. (1981). *Hazardous waste violations: A guide to their detection, investigation and prosecution*. Washington, DC: The National Center on White Collar Crime, Department of Justice, Law Enforcement Assistance Administration.

National Advisory Commission on Criminal Standards and Goals (1976). Washington, DC: Law Enforcement Assistance Administration.

New Jersey Division of Criminal Justice, 2014, Regional Associations Information Network, 2014.

Organized Crime and Hazardous Waste Disposal (1980). Hearing before the Subcommittee on Oversight and Investigations of the Committee on Interstate and Foreign Commerce House of Representatives, 96th Congress, December 16, 1980. Washington, DC: Government Printing Office.

Orr, S. (1989, January 1). Reports criticize EPA for superfund delays and failure to bill polluters. *The Star Ledger*, p. 9.

Orr, S. (1988, November 3). Reagan enacts law to track med waste. *The Star Ledger*, p. 1.

Orr, S. (1990, April 25). Research, prosecution pushed in pollution fight. *The Star Ledger*.

Pecar, J. (1981). Ecological offenses and criminology. *Review Criminal* 32(1): 33–45.

Periconi, J. (2009). The state of environmental prosecution in New York. *Natural Resources and Environment*, 23(3), 11–16.

Porman, M. (1972). *Payoff—The role of organized crime in American politics*. New York: David McKay.

Profile of Organized Crime: Mid-Atlantic Region (1983). Hearings before the Permanent Subcommittee on Governmental Affairs, United States Senate, 98th Congress, February 15, 23, and 24, 1983. Washington, DC: Government Printing Office.

Rast, B. (1989, July 10). Economic summit to focus on environment. *Newhouse News Service*.

Rebovich, D. (May 1986). *Hazardous waste crime: A contextual analysis of the offense and the offender* (Ph.D. diss., Rutgers University). Ann Arbor, MI: University Microfilms International.

Rebovich, D. (1986, June). *Understanding hazardous waste crime: A multi-state examination of offense and offender characteristics in the Northeast*. Trenton: The Northeast Hazardous Waste Project, N.J. Division of Criminal Justice.

Reimers, R. (1985). Emerging technologies of hazardous waste. *In Source Reduction of Hazardous Waste*. Trenton: N.J. Department of Environmental Protection.

Reuter, P. (1982). The value of a bad reputation: Cartels, criminals and barriers to entry. *The Rand Paper Series*. Washington, DC: The Rand Corp.

Reuter, P. (1983). *Disorganized crime: The economics of the visible hand*. Cambridge, MA: MIT Press.

Reuter, P. (1985). Racketeers as cartel organizers. In H. Alexander and G. Carden (eds.), *The politics and economics of organized crime*. Lexington, MA: Lexington Books.

Reuter, P., J. Rubenstein, and S. Wynn (1983). *Racketeering in legitimate industries: Two case studies* (executive summary). Washington, DC: U.S. Department of Justice, National Institute of Justice.

Reuters (2013, September 11). Exxon Mobil unit charged for Pennsylvania fracking waste spill. New York.

Robertson, C. and C. Kraus (2014, September 4). BP May Be Fined Up to $18 Billion for Spill in Gulf. *The New York Times*.

Robillard, R. (1974). Personal interview with a New Jersey deputy attorney general.

Rudolph, R. (1988, March 21). A clean Jersey: U.S. targets environmental crimes. *The Star Ledger*, p. 1.

Sarokin, D. J., W. R. Muir, G. G. Miller, and S. R. Sperber (1985). *Cutting chemical wastes: What 29 organic chemical plants are doing to reduce hazardous wastes*. New York: Inform Inc.

Schmidt, W. (1983, February, 25). Denver lawyer's role in EPA decisions is focus of inquiries by Congress. *The New York Times*, p. 12.

Scholz, J. T. (1984). Cooperation, deterrence, and the ecology of regulatory enforcement. *Law and Society Review* 18(2): 179–224.

Severo, R. (1989, January 9). In war against corrosion, costly by-product is waste. *The New York Times*, p. B1.

Shabecoff, P. (1983, March 16). Shever says EPA aide let Dow delete dioxin tie in draft report. *The New York Times*, p. 1.

Shabecoff, P. (1983, May 11). Internal EPA review criticizes waste cleanup as mismanaged. *The New York Times*, p. 1.

Shabecoff, P. (1983, August 31). Hazardous waste exceeds estimates. *The New York Times*, pp. A1 and A18.

Schelling, T. (1970). Economics and criminal enterprise. In M.E. Wolfgang, L. Savitz & N. Johnston (eds.), *The sociology of crime and delinquency*. New York: John Wiley and Sons, Inc.

Sherman, R. (1987). Pillars or polluters: Prosecutors play hardball with corporate managers, *The New Jersey Law Journal* 6 August: 1.

Shuman, H., and S. Presser (1981). *Questions and answers in attitude surveys: Experiments on question form, wording and context*. New York: Academic Press.

Smith. D. (1980). Paragons, pariahs and pirates: A spectrum-based theory of enterprise. *Crime and Delinquency* 26(3).

Sparks, R. (1979). White-collar crime: The problem and the federal response. In *White collar crime: Hearings before the Subcommittee on Crime of the Committee on the Judiciary House of Representatives, Ninety-Fifth Congress* (serial no. 69). Washington, DC: Government Printing Office.

Sparks, R., A., Greer and S. Manning (1982). *Theoretical studies project final report*. Newark, NJ: Center for the Study of the Causes of Crime for Gain, School of Criminal Justice, Rutgers University.

Stewart, R. B. (1975). The reformation of American administrative law. *Harvard Law Review* 88: 1667–1813.

Stinchcombe, A. L. (1965). Social structure and organizations. In J.G. March (ed.), *Handbook of organizations*. Chicago: Rand McNally.

Stone, C. (1975). *Where the law ends: The social control of corporate behavior*. New York: Harper & Row.

Sullivan, J. (1985, December 15). Trenton panel subpoenas general and E.P.A. aide on pollution by military. *The New York Times*, section 11, pp. 1 and 12.

Sutherland, E. H. (1937). *The professional thief*. Chicago: University of Chicago Press.

Sutherland, E. H. (1961). *White collar crime* (rev. ed.). New York: Holt, Rhinehart, & Winston.

Sutherland, E. H., and D.R. Cressey (1970). *Criminology*. New York: Lippincott.

Swaigen, J. and G. Bunt (1985). *Sentencing in environmental cases*. Ottawa: Law Reform Commission of Canada.

Szasz, A. (1986). Corporations, organized crime, and the disposal of hazardous waste: An examination of the making of a criminogenic regulatory structure. *Criminology* 24(1): 1–28.

Thompson, B. (2010, March 15) PA Dentist, Not NYC Responsible for This Medical Waste on Beach. *NBC News*.

U.S. Environmental Protection Agency (7 August 1978). *Environmental pollution and cancer and heart and lung disease*. First Annual Report to Congress by the Task Force on Environmental Cancer and Heart and Lung Disease.

U.S. Department of Justice (2013, January 28). Walmart pleads guilty to federal environmental crimes.Admits civil violations, and will pay more than $81 million. U.S. Office of Public Affairs.

Vaughan, D. (1982). Toward understanding unlawful organizational behavior. *Michigan Law Review* 80: 1377–1402.

Vaughan, D. (1983). *Controlling unlawful organizational behavior: Social structure and corporate misconduct*. Chicago: University of Chicago Press.

Venezia, J. (1990, February 21). Environmental prosecutor sworn, vows prison for those who pollute. *The Star Ledger*, p. 13.

Weisman, S.R. (1983, February 22). Reagan nominates first EPA chief to head it again. *The New York Times*, p. 1.

Westat Inc. (1984). National survey of hazardous waste generators and treatment, storage and disposal facilities regulated under RCRA in 1981. Washington, DC: Environmental Protection Agency, Office of Solid Waste.

Wolf, S. (1983). Hazardous waste trials and tribulations. *Environmental Law* 13(2).

Yeager, M. G. (1973, Spring). Gangster as white collar criminal—Organized crime and stolen securities. In *Issues in criminology*. Berkeley: University of California.

Index

Index

CPSIA information can be obtained
at www.ICGtesting.com
Printed in the USA
BVHW07s0803180918
527788BV00009B/195/P

9 781412 856010